W9-ARN-114

Sexual Violence

Opposing Viewpoints®

Sexual Violence

Opposing Viewpoints®

Other Books of Related Interest

Sexual Violence

Opposing Viewpoints®

Helen Cothran, *Book Editor*

Daniel Leone, *President*
Bonnie Szumski, *Publisher*
Scott Barbour, *Managing Editor*

OPPOSING
VIEWPOINTS®
SERIES

GREENHAVEN
PRESS®

THOMSON
—————★—————™
GALE

San Diego • Detroit • New York • San Francisco • Cleveland
New Haven, Conn. • Waterville, Maine • London • Munich

LIBRARY OF CONGRESS CATALOGING-IN-PUBLICATION DATA

Sexual violence : opposing viewpoints / Helen Cothran, book editor.
p. cm. — (Opposing viewpoints series)
Includes bibliographical references and index.
ISBN 0-7377-1240-6 (lib. : alk. paper) — ISBN 0-7377-1239-2 (pbk. : alk. paper)
1. Sex crimes. 2. Rape. I. Cothran, Helen. II. Opposing viewpoints series.
HV6556 .S45 2003
364.15'3—dc21   2002034728

Printed in the United States of America

> "Congress shall make
> no law... abridging the
> freedom of speech, or of
> the press."

First Amendment to the U.S. Constitution

The basic foundation of our democracy is the First
Amendment guarantee of freedom of expression.
The Opposing Viewpoints Series is dedicated to the
concept of this basic freedom and the idea that it is
more important to practice it than to enshrine it.

Contents

Why Consider Opposing Viewpoints?

"The only way in which a human being can make some approach to knowing the whole of a subject is by hearing what can be said about it by persons of every variety of opinion and studying all modes in which it can be looked at by every character of mind. No wise man ever acquired his wisdom in any mode but this."

John Stuart Mill

In our media-intensive culture it is not difficult to find differing opinions. Thousands of newspapers and magazines and dozens of radio and television talk shows resound with differing points of view. The difficulty lies in deciding which opinion to agree with and which "experts" seem the most credible. The more inundated we become with differing opinions and claims, the more essential it is to hone critical reading and thinking skills to evaluate these ideas. Opposing Viewpoints books address this problem directly by presenting stimulating debates that can be used to enhance and teach these skills. The varied opinions contained in each book examine many different aspects of a single issue. While examining these conveniently edited opposing views, readers can develop critical thinking skills such as the ability to compare and contrast authors' credibility, facts, argumentation styles, use of persuasive techniques, and other stylistic tools. In short, the Opposing Viewpoints Series is an ideal way to attain the higher-level thinking and reading skills so essential in a culture of diverse and contradictory opinions.

In addition to providing a tool for critical thinking, Opposing Viewpoints books challenge readers to question their own strongly held opinions and assumptions. Most people form their opinions on the basis of upbringing, peer pressure, and personal, cultural, or professional bias. By reading carefully balanced opposing views, readers must directly confront new ideas as well as the opinions of those with whom they disagree. This is not to simplistically argue that everyone who reads opposing views will—or should—change his or her opinion. Instead, the series enhances readers' understanding of their own views by encouraging confrontation with opposing ideas. Careful examination of others' views can lead to the readers' understanding of the logical inconsistencies in their own opinions, perspective on why they hold an opinion, and the consideration of the possibility that their opinion requires further evaluation.

Evaluating Other Opinions

To ensure that this type of examination occurs, Opposing Viewpoints books present all types of opinions. Prominent spokespeople on different sides of each issue as well as well-known professionals from many disciplines challenge the reader. An additional goal of the series is to provide a forum for other, less known, or even unpopular viewpoints. The opinion of an ordinary person who has had to make the decision to cut off life support from a terminally ill relative, for example, may be just as valuable and provide just as much insight as a medical ethicist's professional opinion. The editors have two additional purposes in including these less known views. One, the editors encourage readers to respect others' opinions—even when not enhanced by professional credibility. It is only by reading or listening to and objectively evaluating others' ideas that one can determine whether they are worthy of consideration. Two, the inclusion of such viewpoints encourages the important critical thinking skill of objectively evaluating an author's credentials and bias. This evaluation will illuminate an author's reasons for taking a particular stance on an issue and will aid in readers' evaluation of the author's ideas.

It is our hope that these books will give readers a deeper understanding of the issues debated and an appreciation of the complexity of even seemingly simple issues when good and honest people disagree. This awareness is particularly important in a democratic society such as ours in which people enter into public debate to determine the common good. Those with whom one disagrees should not be regarded as enemies but rather as people whose views deserve careful examination and may shed light on one's own.

Thomas Jefferson once said that "difference of opinion leads to inquiry, and inquiry to truth." Jefferson, a broadly educated man, argued that "if a nation expects to be ignorant and free . . . it expects what never was and never will be." As individuals and as a nation, it is imperative that we consider the opinions of others and examine them with skill and discernment. The Opposing Viewpoints Series is intended to help readers achieve this goal.

David L. Bender and Bruno Leone,
Founders

Greenhaven Press anthologies primarily consist of previously published material taken from a variety of sources, including periodicals, books, scholarly journals, newspapers, government documents, and position papers from private and public organizations. These original sources are often edited for length and to ensure their accessibility for a young adult audience. The anthology editors also change the original titles of these works in order to clearly present the main thesis of each viewpoint and to explicitly indicate the opinion presented in the viewpoint. These alterations are made in consideration of both the reading and comprehension levels of a young adult audience. Every effort is made to ensure that Greenhaven Press accurately reflects the original intent of the authors included in this anthology.

Introduction

"The minimum number of African slaves transported [to the United States] was between 5 million and 6 million. There is no doubt that world trafficking [in sex slaves] now is around that number."
—Laura Lederer of the Protection Project at Johns Hopkins University School of Advanced International Studies

When Pia Agustin Corvera turned nine, her aunt, who had been raising her in a Manila, Philippines, slum, began selling her to foreign men for three dollars a sexual encounter. At twelve, Pia was sold to a visiting German pedophile. Finally, at age sixteen, Pia found refuge in a therapeutic community for child victims of sexual abuse located in the Philippines. Succinctly describing her experience, Pia says, "I felt like garbage."

Unfortunately, Pia is not alone. According to Ron O'Grady, honorary president of ECPAT (End Child Prostitution in Asian Tourism) International, "Today, child sex abuse is far more prevalent than anyone had realized.... For the first time in history, social workers, law enforcement officers and governments have initiated a series of investigations into this previously hidden aspect of society." The U.S. State Department estimates that 2 million women and children are trafficked globally and more than 50,000 women are sold into U.S. brothels. The European Union has estimated that Western Europe illegally imports 500,000 prostitutes a year. The Thai government reports that 60,000 Thai children are sold into prostitution each year.

Sexual trafficking is not only widespread but extremely lucrative. While Pia's aunt received a mere three dollars for every sexual act Pia engaged in, international sex trafficking brings in from 7 to 12 billion dollars of revenue annually. Janis Gordon, assistant U.S. attorney for the Organized Crime Strike Force in Atlanta, Georgia, claims that "after examining one brothel's records, I was able to show that it grossed 1.5 million dollars over a two-year period." Republican senator Sam Brownback from Kansas claims that "human trafficking is the third-highest illegal-income source in America today behind drug- and gunrunning." The increase in profits from sexual trafficking has led to the worldwide growth of organized crime, the primary beneficiary of the international sex trade.

Sexual trafficking is defined as the movement of women and children, usually from one nation to another, but sometimes within a nation, for purposes of prostitution or sexual servitude and slavery. While Asian nations, especially Japan, have traditionally been the largest source of female and child prostitutes, with the breakup of the Soviet Union and the region's resultant economic woes, the world's sex slaves are increasingly coming from Eastern Europe. According to columnist Robert Scheer, "In Ukraine, the sale of women by international gangsters is becoming the new nation's most lucrative export." Girls in Russian orphanages often become victims of sex traffickers because they lack the basic resources for survival. Six out of ten Russian female orphans fall prey to traffickers.

Sex trafficking in Eastern Europe highlights the key reason that women and children become sex slaves: poverty. Families sell their young children to get money, and struggling women prostitute themselves when all other options for earning income fail. Moreover, an overall increase in poverty in developing nations and the mounting power of criminal mafias has exacerbated the problem. Another factor that has led to an increase in child sex trafficking is the AIDS epidemic. Whereas in the past those who sought out children for sexual encounters were primarily pedophiles, many of today's purchasers of sex from children are men worried about contracting AIDS from unfamiliar sexual partners. Children, they assume, would be free of AIDS.

Many experts agree that globalization and the Internet are important contributors to the sex trade as well. As tourism in general has increased as a result of globalization, so too has sexual trafficking. Initially "sex tourism" took the form of Japanese and American male tourists joining group tours whose function was to provide sexual adventures in Asian nations. Such overt tour groups no longer operate, but organized networks of tourist pedophiles still exist. They share information on the best countries to visit in order to find child sex slaves.

The Internet has made sex tourism much easier to conduct. The anonymous nature of the Net makes it safer for pedophiles from around the world to communicate with one another. The Internet also provides a medium for the easy sharing of photographs and video of child abuse, which experts say fuels further abusive acts. Finally, pedophiles can use the Net to lure unsuspecting children into sexual online conversations and to arrange for actual meetings where abuse will take place.

With globalization and the Internet increasing the sex trade, international and domestic entities have begun developing possible solutions to the problem. For example, in 1989, the United Nations adopted the UN Convention on the Rights of the Child. When nations sign the Convention, they are implicitly agreeing with what O'Grady calls "the revolutionary concept that each child born into the world is endowed with inalienable rights." According to O'Grady, children have historically been viewed as property. The UN Convention changes that: Children now have the same rights as other disenfranchised minorities. Proponents of the document hope that this shift in attitude will propel nations into combating sex trafficking.

Perhaps the most effective solution to the sex trade to date is the Victims of Trafficking and Violence Protection Act of 2000. This U.S. law requires the State Department to expand its annual human-rights reports to cover severe forms of trafficking in persons. In addition, an interagency task force will coordinate antitrafficking efforts nationally and internationally. Brownback says of the law, "The biggest thing this law does is say to the world that the United States sees this as a serious human-rights issue. It raises public awareness about the dangers of trafficking and the protections available for victims."

Whether the actions being taken by concerned entities to combat sex trafficking will ultimately prevent the kind of personal devastation that Pia Agustin Corvera experienced in the Philippines remains to be seen. Solutions to social problems such as sexual exploitation that have deep roots—in this case, widespread poverty—can prove insufficient. The authors in *Sexual Violence: Opposing Viewpoints* debate the causes of and solutions to sexual exploitation in the following chapters: What Causes Sexual Violence? Is Sexual Violence a Serious Problem? How Should Society Address Sexual Victimization? How Can Sexual Violence Be Reduced? Prominent on the radar screens of those concerned about sexual violence will certainly be the increasing prevalence of sex trafficking.

CHAPTER 1

What Causes Sexual Violence?

Chapter Preface

In 1992 professional boxer Mike Tyson was convicted of raping eighteen-year-old beauty queen Desiree Washington. The Tyson trial is one of many high-profile cases involving professional athletes accused of sexual misconduct. Such cases have generated questions about why male athletes tend to assault women with more frequency than do other men. Nancy Scannell, director of public policy for the Massachusetts Coalition Against Sexual Assault and Domestic Violence, says of Mike Tyson, "Here's a man who makes a living beating people up, and then we're astonished when he forces sex on someone!" To analysts such as Scannell, the violent nature of many sports—especially boxing, football, and hockey—encourages violent behavior. Other theories abound to explain the high incidence of abuse by male sports figures.

While misconduct by professional athletes seems to garner the most media attention, sexual assault by college athletes has generated the most scholarly scrutiny. For example, a 1995 study of ten Division I colleges found that while athletes made up just 3.3 percent of the student body, they were responsible for 19 percent of all sexual assaults reported to campus authorities. Another study found that in twenty-two of the twenty-four cases of gang rapes on campus the perpetrators were members of fraternities or athletic teams. A study conducted by Mary Koss and John Gaines of the University of Arizona found that male college students who participated in formal athletics were slightly more hostile toward women and more likely to engage in sexual aggression. Some researchers have postulated that organized athletics shield men from the consequences of their actions. Others speculate that male athletes sexually assault women in order to prove their masculinity to other team members and dispel any suggestions that they might be homosexual. Some analysts believe that rampant alcohol abuse by campus athletes plays a role in sexual aggression.

No studies have been conducted on the sexual abuse of children by coaches, but anecdotal evidence suggests that such abuse is a serious problem. In one high-profile case, reported in the 1997 spring issue of *Sports Illustrated*, Rick Butler, coach at the Sports Performance Volleyball Club in West Chicago, Illinois, allegedly sexually abused at least three of his teenage volleyball players. Analysts say that similar incidents are disturbingly common because of the unbalanced relationship between coach and athlete in youth sports. In organized athletics, a respected authority figure is in frequent contact with trusting minors. The coach is typically male, older, and physically bigger and stronger than the abused athlete, who is usually female, younger, and weaker.

Theories that explain why sports seem to encourage sexual abuse continue to be investigated. The violent nature of some sports, the protective fraternity of male athletes, and the trusting relationship between coach and athlete all have been proposed as explanations for the high incidence of abuse in sports. In the following chapter, authors debate other proposed causes of sexual violence, such as pornography and traditional gender roles. Discovering why sexual violence occurs can help experts prevent the devastation experienced by abuse victims.

*"Rape has evolved over millennia of human
history, along with courtship, sexual
attraction and other behaviors related to
the production of offspring."*

Rape Is a Natural Biological Act

Randy Thornhill and Craig T. Palmer

Randy Thornhill is an evolutionary biologist at the University of New Mexico in Albuquerque. Craig T. Palmer is an evolutionary anthropologist at the University of Colorado at Colorado Springs. In the following viewpoint, adapted from their book *A Natural History of Rape: Biological Bases of Sexual Coercion*, the authors contend that rape evolved as a male reproductive strategy. According to Thornhill and Palmer, females are choosy about mates because sexual reproduction exacts such high costs in terms of pregnancy, childbirth, and child rearing. In response, the authors maintain, males developed several sexual strategies to win females' attention. They circumvent female choice through rape when other strategies fail.

As you read, consider the following questions:
1. What facts do the authors provide as evidence that rape is a natural, biological phenomenon?
2. According to Thornhill and Palmer, what do social scientists believe causes rape?
3. What two ways other than rape can men gain access to women?

The quest for the answer to [the question of why men rape] has occupied the two of us collectively for more than forty years. As a purely scientific puzzle, the problem is hard enough. But it is further roiled by strong ideological currents. Many social theorists view rape not only as an ugly crime but as a symptom of an unhealthy society, in which men fear and disrespect women. In 1975 the feminist writer Susan Brownmiller asserted that rape is motivated not by lust but by the urge to control and dominate. In the twenty-five years since, Brownmiller's view has become mainstream. All men feel sexual desire, the theory goes, but not all men rape. Rape is viewed as an unnatural behavior that has nothing to do with sex, and one that has no corollary in the animal world.

Undoubtedly, individual rapists may have a variety of motivations. A man may rape because, for instance, he wants to impress his friends by losing his virginity, or because he wants to avenge himself against a woman who has spurned him. But social scientists have not convincingly demonstrated that rapists are not at least partly motivated by sexual desire as well. Indeed, how could a rape take place at all without sexual motivation on the part of the rapist? Isn't sexual arousal of the rapist the one common factor in all rapes, including date rapes, rapes of children, rapes of women under anesthetic and even gang rapes committed by soldiers during war?

Rape Is About Sex

We want to challenge the dearly held idea that rape is not about sex. We realize that our approach and our frankness will rankle some social scientists, including some serious and well-intentioned rape investigators. But many facts point to the conclusion that rape is, in its very essence, a sexual act. Furthermore, we argue, rape has evolved over millennia of human history, along with courtship, sexual attraction and other behaviors related to the production of offspring.

Consider the following facts:
• Most rape victims are women of childbearing age.
• In many cultures rape is treated as a crime against the victim's husband.

- Rape victims suffer less emotional distress when they are subjected to more violence.
- Rape takes place not only among human beings but also in a variety of other animal species.
- Married women and women of childbearing age experience more psychological distress after a rape than do girls, single women or women who are past menopause.

As bizarre as some of those facts may seem, they all make sense when rape is viewed as a natural, biological phenomenon that is a product of the human evolutionary heritage.

Here we must hasten to emphasize that by categorizing a behavior as "natural" and "biological" we do not in any way mean to imply that the behavior is justified or even inevitable. Biological means "of or pertaining to life," so the word applies to every human feature and behavior. But to infer from that—as many of our critics assert that we do—that what is biological is somehow right or good, would be to fall into the so-called naturalistic fallacy. That mistake is obvious enough when one considers such natural disasters as epidemics, floods and tornadoes. In those cases it is clear that what is natural is not always desirable. And of course much can be, and is, done to protect people against natural threats—from administering antibiotics to drawing up emergency evacuation plans. In other words, the fact that rape is an ancient part of human nature in no way excuses the rapist.

A Deep Schism

Why, then, have the editors of scholarly journals refused to publish papers that treat rape from a Darwinian perspective [pertaining to the ideas of naturalist Charles Darwin]? Why have pickets and audience protesters caused public lectures on the evolutionary basis of rape to be canceled or terminated? Why have investigators working to discover the evolutionary causes of rape been denied positions at universities?

The reason is the deep schism between many social scientists and investigators such as ourselves who are proponents of what is variously called sociobiology or evolutionary psychology. Social scientists regard culture—everything from eating habits to language—as an entirely human invention, one that develops arbitrarily. According to that view, the desires of men and women are learned behaviors. Rape takes place only when men learn to rape, and it can be eradicated simply by substituting new lessons. Sociobiologists, by contrast, emphasize that learned behavior, and indeed all culture, is the result of psychological adaptations that have evolved over long periods of time. Those adaptations, like all traits of individual human beings, have both genetic and environmental components. We fervently believe that, just as the leopard's spots and the giraffe's elongated neck are the result of aeons of past Darwinian selection, so also is rape.

Not a Uniquely Human Phenomenon

One factor recommending the significance of biology to understanding rape is that forced copulation is by no means a uniquely human phenomenon. The behavior is widely documented, in both wild and laboratory conditions, in species ranging from our closest primate relatives (including orangutans, chimpanzees, and gorillas) to more distant primates, other mammals, birds, and insects. Typically, the existence of common behaviors between humans and other creatures (such as sexual desire, care of offspring, and the like), just as the existence of common structures (opposable thumbs, four limbs, and the like), recommends the consideration of common origins. . . .

In addition to the mere fact that males of many species besides humans force copulations, it is significant that the patterns in which rape occurs in humans are often strikingly similar to the patterns of rape behavior in the other animal species in which rape occurs.

Owen D. Jones, *Hastings Women's Law Journal*, Summer 2000.

That conclusion has profound and immediate practical consequences. The rape-prevention measures that are being taught to police officers, lawyers, parents, college students and potential rapists are based on the prevailing social-science view, and are therefore doomed to fail. The Darwinian theory of evolution by natural selection is the most powerful scientific theory that applies to living things. As long as efforts to prevent rape remain uninformed by that theory, they will continue to be handicapped by ideas about human nature that are fundamentally inadequate. We believe that only by acknowledging the evolutionary roots of rape can prevention tactics be devised that really work.

Sexual Costs: Different for Men and Women

From a Darwinian perspective, every kind of animal—whether grasshopper or gorilla, German or Ghanaian—has evolved to produce healthy children that will survive to pass along their parents' genetic legacy. The mechanics of the phenomenon are simple: animals born without traits that led to reproduction died out, whereas the ones that reproduced the most succeeded in conveying their genes to posterity. Crudely speaking, sex feels good because over evolutionary time the animals that liked having sex created more offspring than the animals that didn't. . . .

Over vast periods of evolutionary time, men and women have confronted quite different reproductive challenges. Whereas fathers can share the responsibilities of child rearing, they do not have to. Like most of their male counterparts in the rest of the animal kingdom, human males can reproduce successfully with a minimal expenditure of time and energy; once the brief act of sexual intercourse is completed, their contribution can cease. By contrast, the minimum effort required for a woman to reproduce successfully includes nine months of pregnancy and a painful childbirth. Typically, ancestral females also had to devote themselves to prolonged breastfeeding and many years of child care if they were to ensure the survival of their genes. In short, a man can have many children, with little inconvenience to himself; a woman can have only a few, and with great effort.

That difference is the key to understanding the origins of certain important adaptations—features that persist because they were favored by natural selection in the past. Given the low cost in time and energy that mating entails for the male, selection favored males who mated frequently. By contrast, selection favored females who gave careful consideration to their choice of a mate; that way, the high costs of mating for the female would be undertaken under circumstances that were most likely to produce healthy offspring. The result is that men show greater interest than women do in having a variety of sexual partners and in having casual sex without investment or commitment. That commonplace observation has been confirmed by many empirical studies. . . .

Choosy Women and Eager Men

Since women are choosy, men have been selected for finding a way to be chosen. One way to do that is to possess traits that women prefer: men with symmetrical body features are attractive to women, presumably because such features are a sign of health. A second way that men can gain access to women is by defeating other men in fights or other kinds of competitions—thereby gaining power, resources and social status, other qualities that women find attractive.

Rape can be understood as a third kind of sexual strategy: one more way to gain access to females. There are several mechanisms by which such a strategy could function. For example, men might resort to rape when they are socially disenfranchised, and thus unable to gain access to women through looks, wealth or status. Alternatively, men could have evolved to practice rape when the costs seem low—when, for instance, a woman is alone and unprotected (and thus retaliation seems unlikely), or when they have physical control over a woman (and so cannot be injured by her). Over evolutionary time, some men may have succeeded in passing on their genes through rape, thus perpetuating the behavior. It is also possible, however, that rape evolved not as a reproductive strategy in itself but merely as a side effect of other adaptations, such as the strong male sex drive and the male desire to mate with a variety of women. . . .

Eradicating Rape

Unlike many other contentious social issues, such as abortion and homosexual rights, everyone has the same goal regarding rape: to end it. Evolutionary biology provides clear information that society can use to achieve that goal. Social science, by contrast, promotes erroneous solutions, because it fails to recognize that Darwinian selection has shaped not only human bodies but human psychology, learning patterns and behavior as well. The fact is that men, relative to women, are more aggressive, sexually assertive and eager to copulate, and less discriminating about mates—traits that contribute to the existence of rape. When social scientists mistakenly assert that socialization alone causes those gender differences, they ignore the fact that the same differences also exist in all the other animal species in which males offer less parental investment than females and compete for access to females.

In addressing the question of rape, the choice between the politically constructed answers of social science and the evidentiary answers of evolutionary biology is essentially a choice between ideology and knowledge. As scientists who would like to see rape eradicated from human life, we sincerely hope that truth will prevail.

"*[The theory] that the rapist isn't a psychopath, just an ordinary fellow who's in touch with his inner caveman, leads to some dubious prescriptions.*"

Rape Is Not a Natural Biological Act

Barbara Ehrenreich

Barbara Ehrenreich argues in the following viewpoint that the theory that men rape due to a natural biological urge to procreate is based on faulty reasoning. For one thing, Ehrenreich points out, since the child produced by the rapist would have no male parent, the chances of its survival would be greatly reduced. Moreover, she reasons that the child's chance of success would be further decreased because its mother would likely be damaged by the rape, making her a less than ideal parent. Since the child produced by rape would have a limited chance of surviving, Ehrenreich concludes, the desire to procreate cannot be considered the cause of rape. Barbara Ehrenreich is a writer, activist, and novelist whose work appears in many publications.

As you read, consider the following questions:
1. On what fact do Randy Thornhill and Craig T. Palmer base their theory that rape is motivated by lust and the desire to procreate, according to the author?
2. As stated by Ehrenreich, what is a male's "parental investment"?
3. How does the author refute the claim by Thornhill and Palmer that how women dress influences their likelihood of being raped?

Barbara Ehrenreich, "How 'Natural' Is Rape? Despite a Daffy New Theory, It's Not Just a Guy in Touch with His Inner Caveman," *Time*, vol. 155, January 31, 2000, p. 88. Copyright © 2000 by Time, Inc. Reproduced by permission.

It was cute the first time around: when President [Bill Clinton] lost his head over [White House aide] Monica Lewinsky's thong undies [during the Monica Lewinsky scandal in the 1990s], that is, and the evolutionary psychologists declared that he was just following the innate biological urge to, tee-hee, spread his seed. Natural selection favors the reproductively gifted, right? But the latest daffy Darwinist attempt to explain male bad behavior is not quite so amusing. Rape, according to evolutionary theorists Randy Thornhill and Craig T. Palmer, represents just another seed-spreading technique favored by natural selection. Sure it's nasty, brutish and short on foreplay. But it gets the job done.

Thornhill and Palmer aren't endorsing rape, of course. In their article in the latest issue of the *Sciences*—which is already generating a high volume of buzz although their book, *A Natural History of Rape*, won't be out until April [2000]— they say they just want to correct the feminist fallacy that "rape is not about sex," it's about violence and domination. The authors argue, among other things, that since the majority of victims are women of childbearing age, the motive must be lust and the intent, however unconscious, must be to impregnate. Hence rape is not an act of pathology, but a venerable old strategy for procreation. What's "natural" isn't always nice.

Now, there are people who reject any attempt to apply evolutionary theory to human behavior, and, as far as I'm concerned, they can go back to composing their annual letters to Santa Claus. Obviously, humans have been shaped by natural selection (though it's not always so obvious how). We are not the descendants of the kindest or wisest of hominids—only of those who managed, by cunning or luck, to produce a few living offspring. But is rape really an effective strategy for guys who, deep down in their genes, just want to be fruitful and multiply?

There are plenty of evolutionary psychologists who would answer with a resounding no. They emphasize the evolutionary value of the human male's "parental investment"—his tendency to stick around after the act of impregnation and help out with the kids. Prehistoric dads may not have read many bed-time stories, but, in this account, they very likely brought home the occasional antelope haunch, and they almost certainly played a major role in defending the family from four-legged predators. In contrast, the rapist generally operates on a hit-and-run basis—which may be all right for stocking sperm banks, but is not quite so effective if the goal is to produce offspring who will survive in a challenging environment. The children of guys who raped-and-ran must have been a scrawny lot and doomed to end up on some leopard's lunch menu.

The Dangers of Biological Interpretations

Biology, applied to human behavior [such as rape], has a disturbing history of misuse. College students in introductory courses are taught the perils of "social Darwinism," a 19th-century theory that borrowed catch words of evolutionary thinking and twisted them into a justification for class differences: the struggle for wealth and power, social Darwinists argued, was a battle for "survival of the fittest," a term coined by Herbert Spencer, an English philosopher.

Darwin's theory, stretched and distorted in various ways, was also called upon by the Nazis as a rationale for genocide, and has been a staple of forced sterilization campaigns and racist propaganda.

In the decades after World War II, the record of these abuses created a distrust of biological explanations for human behavior.

Erica Goode, *New York Times*, March 14, 2000.

There's another problem with rape—again, from a strictly Darwinian perspective. Even if it isn't "about violence," as feminists have claimed, it almost always involves violence or at least the threat thereof; otherwise it isn't rape. Thornhill and Palmer downplay the amount of physical violence accompanying rape, claiming that no more than 22% of victims suffer any "gratuitous" violence beyond that necessary to subdue them. But we are still talking about appalling levels of damage to the mother of the rapist's prospective offspring. Most rape victims suffer long-term emotional consequences—like depression and memory loss—that are hardly conducive to successful motherhood. It's a pretty dumb Darwinian specimen who can't plant his seed without breaking the "vessel" in the process.

Thornhill and Palmer's insistence that the rapist isn't a psychopath, just an ordinary fellow who's in touch with his inner caveman, leads to some dubious prescriptions. They want to institute formal training for boys in how to resist their "natural" sexual impulses to rape. Well, sure, kids should learn that rape is wrong, along with all other forms of assault. But the emphasis on rape as a natural male sexual impulse is bound to baffle those boys—and I would like to think there are more than a few of them out there—whose sexual fantasies have never drifted in a rape-ward direction.

As for the girls, Thornhill and Palmer want them to realize that since rape is really "about sex," it very much matters how they dress. But where is the evidence that women in miniskirts are more likely to be raped than women in dirndls? Women were raped by the thousands in Bosnia [during its war with Serbia and Croatia in the 1990s], for example, and few if any of them were wearing bikinis or bustiers.

Yes, rape is "about sex," in that it involves a certain sexlike act. But it's a pretty dismal kind of "sex" in which one person's pain, and possible permanent injury, is the occasion for the other one's pleasure. What most of us mean by sex is something mutual and participatory, loving and uplifting or at least flirty and fun. In fact, making the world safe for plunging necklines and thong undies is a goal that enlightened members of both sexes ought to be able to get behind. As for those guys who can't distinguish between sex and rape, I don't care whether they're as "natural" as granola, they don't deserve to live in the company of women.

31

> "In pornography women exist solely to the end of male pleasure, no matter how degrading, no matter how violent."

Pornography Causes Sexual Violence

Fear Us

In the following viewpoint, the feminist organization Fear Us contends that pornography encourages men to view women as sexual objects to be exploited by men. According to Fear Us, all pornography is implicitly violent and leads to sexual violence against women. The organization argues that women, not the First Amendment rights of pornographers, should be protected.

As you read, consider the following questions:
1. In the organization's view, how are prostitution and pornography similar?
2. In what two fields do women make more money than men, according to the organization?
3. As stated by Fear Us, how are magazines like *Playboy* and *Penthouse* implicitly violent?

Prostitution is illegal in every state except Nevada; why then is pornography legal? What is the difference if a woman gets paid to perform an act of sex, or if she gets paid to perform an act of sex in front of a camera? How does a camera "legitimatize" the act? Both women are engaging in sex for pay. Is one woman a prostitute and the other a porn "star" because society values the product rather than the act or the woman? These are the 10 billion dollar a year questions that no one seems to be able to answer.

Violence and Exploitation

A woman's average income is typically 73% of the wages a man will earn for the same job. There are, however, two exceptions: women earn more money than men in the fields of modeling and pornography/prostitution. These areas, society tells us, are where a woman's value lies. So in the last few decades women have become socialized to view themselves as sexual objects and Supermodels and porn "stars" have become role models for our young girls. We have become so used to seeing the media violate and exploit women that we no longer recognize it as violence or exploitation.

The falsehood that pornography is "harmless" and is to be protected as "free speech" ignores the fact that every act depicted in pornography is acted out on a real woman, a woman whose only purpose is about the same as that of a spittoon. The abuse pornographers inflict on women in the act of making pornography is not a thought, an idea, a fantasy or speech; it is corporeal. This distortion also ignores the research in aggression that finds the relationship between sexually violent images in the media and changes in or toward callous attitudes toward women is stronger statistically than the relationship between smoking and cancer.

Pornography is a ten billion dollar a year industry. Ten billion dollars a year is more than the television and movie industry combined. And because these profits matter and women do not, because pornographers have rights and powerful friends and women do not, because the first amendment matters and women do not, because these pictures and movies are important and women are not, the products of pornography are protected, and women are not.

In a study done in Vancouver [British Columbia, Canada] of all the sexually aggressive scenes [in non-X-rated pornography], it was found that:

- 46% involved bondage or confinement
- 23% involved slapping, hitting, spanking or pulling hair
- 22% involved rape
- 18% involved sexual harassment
- 4% involved sadomasochism
- 3% involved sexual mutilation

Timmons and Area Women in Crisis, http://crisis.vianet.on.ca.

Women as Passive Partners in Their Own Exploitation

Pornographers often portray women asking for their own violation, torture and even murder.

Pregnant women, lactating women, women having sex with animals, men raping and urinating on women—all are on display for the sexual gratification of men.

The messages people receive from pornography are that women are passive, even willing, partners in their own exploitation, and that men are entitled to unconditional use of women's bodies for their own pleasure. In pornography, women's sexuality and behavior is defined by men who feel a monetary or divine right to have access to female bodies. Sex is neither a female service nor a male right, but pornography states that it is. Pornography purports to define what a woman is, and in pornography women exist solely to the end of male pleasure, no matter how degrading, no matter how violent.

Pornography that is not overtly violent is still implicitly violent because it objectifies and degrades women. Magazines like *Playboy* and *Penthouse* have as great an impact as hard-core pornography, and the supposed "legitimacy" of these types of magazines diminishes the perceived harm done. Pornography that is glossed over with a patina of "chic" is not art, it is *pornography*.

Pornography steals our sexuality and sells back to us a warped caricature of what it once naturally was. Pornographers do not celebrate female sexuality, they exploit it. Pornography may sometimes be idea, fantasy or speech, but it is always harm. Women's lives, health and safety are more important than men's fantasies, ideas and speech.

Author Marilyn French said, "But it cannot be an accident that everywhere on the globe one sex harms the other so massively that one questions the sanity of those waging the campaign: can a species survive when half of it systematically preys on the other?"

It is past time for humanity to examine its values, change its thinking, and survive.

> *"Demonstrated empirical links between pornography and sex crimes in general are weak or absent."*

Pornography Does Not Cause Sexual Violence

American Civil Liberties Union

The American Civil Liberties Union (ACLU) is a national organization that works to protect Americans' civil rights. In the following viewpoint, the ACLU argues that no correlation exists between pornography and sexual violence against women. Moreover, because female porn stars freely elect to participate in the making of pornography, pornography cannot be said to harm the women involved in making it. The ACLU contends that due to a lack of evidence that pornography harms women, pornography should be considered a form of free speech protected by the First Amendment.

As you read, consider the following questions:
1. How does the ACLU substantiate its assertion that pornography is protected by the First Amendment?
2. What happened as a result of Canada's 1992 Supreme Court obscenity ruling, according to the ACLU?
3. As stated by the organization, in what ways are anti-pornography laws paternalistic?

American Civil Liberties Union, "Why the ACLU Opposes Censorship of 'Pornography,'" www.aclu.org, December 11, 1994. Copyright © 1994 by the American Civil Liberties Union. Reproduced by permission.

S exually explicit material, in literature, art, film, photography and music, has always been controversial in the United States, from James Joyce's *Ulysses*—which was banned in the 1930s—to rap music performed by 2 Live Crew, a target of prosecution in the 1990s. Traditionally, political conservatives and religious fundamentalists have been the primary advocates of tight legal restrictions on sexual expression, based on their view that such expression undermines public morality. In the late 1970s, however, those traditional voices were joined by a small but extremely vocal segment of the feminist movement. These women, who do not by any means speak for all feminists, charge that "pornography" is a major cause of discrimination and violence against women and should, therefore, be suppressed.

Although unsupported by any reliable evidence, this theory has been especially influential on college and law school campuses, leading to several incidents in which speech and works of art—including works by women artists—have been labeled "pornographic" and censored. Even classics like Francisco de Goya's painting, *The Nude Maja*, have been targeted.

The American Civil Liberties Union (ACLU) has fought censorship from the time of its founding in 1920. In our early days, we defended sex educator/activists Margaret Sanger and Mary Ware Dennett against criminal obscenity charges. Today, we continue to defend the free speech rights of all expression, including sexual expression. We believe that the suppression of "pornography" is not only damaging to the First Amendment, but also impedes the struggle for women's rights.

Here are some answers to questions often asked by the public about the ACLU's opposition to the suppression of pornography.

Is Pornography Protected by the First Amendment?

Yes. The First Amendment absolutely forbids the suppression of ideas or images based on their content alone. Moreover, a basic tenet of U.S. Supreme Court jurisprudence is that laws must be "viewpoint" neutral. And even though the Court has carved out a narrow exception to the First Amendment for a category of sexually explicit material deemed "legally obscene," the term "pornography" has no legal significance at all.

The dictionary defines pornography simply as writing or visual images that are "intended to arouse sexual desire." Pro-censorship feminists have greatly expanded the common meaning of pornography, redefining it as "the sexually explicit subordination of women through pictures and/or words." They then define "subordination" as the depiction of women "in postures or positions of sexual submission, servility, or display." These extraordinarily subjective interpretations would apply to everything from religious imagery to news accounts of mass rape in Bosnia. Because the Supreme Court has consistently ruled that the government may not make content-based rules limiting free speech, material that depicts "the subordination of women" enjoys the same First Amendment protection afforded material that depicts women in other ways. Were that not so, the government could suppress any ideas it didn't like, rendering the First Amendment meaningless.

Is Pornography a Form of Discrimination Against Women?

Sexually explicit words and images aimed at arousing sexual desire—pornography—constitute a form of expression. Pro-censorship feminists seek legal recognition of their counter-claim that such images are a form of sex discrimination because they reinforce stereotypes of women as inferior. The architects of the latter concept are law professor Catharine MacKinnon and writer Andrea Dworkin, who drafted a model law that would permit any woman claiming to have been harmed by pornography to bring a civil lawsuit for monetary damages, and to halt the production, distribution and sale of pornographic works.

The model law has been considered in numerous locales around the country, but when it was adopted by the Indianapolis City Council in 1984 it collapsed under a legal challenge brought by a coalition of booksellers and publishers and supported by the ACLU as a friend-of-the-court. Leaving no doubt that the law targeted expression, federal Judge

Sara Barker wrote: "To deny free speech in order to engineer social change in the name of accomplishing a greater good for one sector of our society erodes the freedoms of all and . . . threatens tyranny and injustice for those subjected to the rule of such laws."

People Do Not Mimic What They View

People do not mimic what they read or view in knee-jerk fashion. If they did, the feminist books of the last 25 years would have transformed this into a perfect feminist world. If they did, advertisers could run an ad and consumers would obey. Instead, businesses spend millions of dollars and still, the strongest motive for purchases is price. People juggle words and images—good and bad—with all the others that they have seen or heard, and with all their real life experiences. It is experience that is the strongest teacher.

Men do not learn coercion from pictures of sex.

Feminists for Free Expression, 1993, www.ffe.org.

The ACLU's fears about the censorious effects of the MacKinnon/Dworkin law have been borne out in Canada, where the Canadian Supreme Court incorporated that law's definition of pornography into a 1992 obscenity ruling. Since then, more than half of all feminist bookstores in Canada have had materials confiscated or the sales of some materials suspended by the government. The most susceptible to repression have been stores that specialize in lesbian and gay writings.

Wouldn't Ridding Society of Pornography Reduce Violence Against Women?

Although pro-censorship feminists base their efforts on the assumption that pornography causes violence against women, such a causal relationship has never been established. The National Research Council's Panel on Understanding and Preventing Violence concluded, in a 1993 survey of laboratory studies, that "demonstrated empirical links between pornography and sex crimes in general are weak or absent."

Correlational studies are similarly inconclusive, revealing no consistent correlations between the availability of por-

nography in various communities or countries and sexual offense rates. If anything, studies suggest that a greater availability of pornography seems to correlate with higher in-
dices of sexual equality. Women in Sweden, with its highly
permissive attitudes toward sexual expression, are much
safer and have more civil rights than women in Singapore,
where restrictions on pornography are very tight.

Doesn't Pornography Exploit the Women Who Participate in Its Production?

The ACLU supports the aggressive enforcement of already
existing civil and criminal laws to protect women from sexual violence and coercion in the process of making sexually
oriented material. At the same time, we oppose the notion,
advanced by anti-pornography feminists, that women can
never make free, voluntary choices to participate in the production of pornography, and that they are always coerced,
whether they realize it or not. This infantilization of women
denies them the freedom of choice to engage in otherwise
legal activities.

There are cases of women who say they were coerced into
working in the pornography industry, the most well known
being "Linda Lovelace," who starred in the movie *Deep
Throat*. But the majority of women who pose for sexually explicit material or act in pornographic films do so voluntarily.
Indeed, these women resent attempts to outlaw their chosen
occupation. As one actress exclaimed, "For them to tell me I
can't make films about naked men and women making love
is a grotesque violation of my civil rights."

Do Anti-Pornography Laws Undermine Equality?

A core idea of the anti-pornography movement is the propo-
sition that sex per se degrades women (although not men).
Even consensual, nonviolent sex, according to MacKinnon
and Dworkin, is an evil from which women—like children—
must be protected. Such thinking is a throwback to the archaic stereotypes of the 19th century that formed the basis
for enacting laws to "protect" women from vulgar language
(and from practicing law or sitting on juries lest they be subjected to such language). Paternalistic legislation such as that

advocated by MacKinnon and Dworkin has always functioned to prevent women from achieving full legal equality.

Furthermore, history teaches that censorship is a dangerous weapon in the hands of government. Inevitably, it is used against those who want to change society, be they feminists, civil rights demonstrators or gay liberationists. Obscenity laws, especially, have been used to suppress information and art dealing with female sexuality and reproduction. Thus, the growing influence of anti-pornography feminism threatens to undermine long-established principles of free speech.

Finally, the focus on sexual imagery and symbols diverts attention from the real causes of discrimination and violence against women, as well as from problems such as unequal pay, lack of affordable childcare and sexual harassment in the workplace.

| "Men are trained to rape and women to take it."

Traditional Male/Female Roles Promote Sexual Violence

Alyn Pearson

Alyn Pearson argues in the following viewpoint that men are trained to sexually abuse women, and women are conditioned to accept abuse. According to Pearson, men enjoy social power and privilege at the expense of women, who are brainwashed into giving in to what men want while simultaneously believing that they are treated equally to men. Pearson likens rape to an endemic disease that can only be cured when people are willing to challenge the cultural environment that fosters it. Alyn Pearson has written several articles for *Off Our Backs* magazine.

As you read, consider the following questions:
1. According to Pearson, what is the difference between an endemic disease and an epidemic?
2. What things do women feel they have to do in order to be accepted by men, as stated by the author?
3. According to the author, what solutions to rape does the media suggest?

During the Spring 2000 semester, I filled my undergraduate science requirement with a class called "The Biology of Infectious Diseases." Although all biologically caused, many of the diseases we studied were closely tied to social conditions. For example, in the United States and Europe in the early 1900s, typhoid thrived among rural and urban poor. Typhoid is a disease of the intestines caused by bacteria which result from contamination from sewage or feces. In poor urban and rural areas, water sanitation was poor, so often the septic system and the water supply were intermingled, allowing the bacteria to pass to people. These days, with improved sanitation, typhoid in the United States is relatively scarce, but in countries with poor water sanitation, typhoid is still endemic.

Endemic means "part of the natural flora of a place." In nations with poor water and health care, diseases like typhoid are part of the environment. An endemic disease is not a good thing, but people somehow get used to it and deal accordingly. (An epidemic, on the other hand, is an outbreak, often sudden, of a disease that strikes many people severely.) Endemic diseases, ones that are chronic like rainy weather in the Pacific Northwest, tend to spawn folklore explanations as to their etiology. For example, there is a lot of folklore about the common cold. It is common lore that if we get caught in the rain we are apt to "catch cold," that if we are out too long in the freezing weather, we might "get a chill," and that if we go out in cold weather with wet hair we might "catch a cold."

Rape as Disease

Rape is the common cold of society. Although rape is much more serious than the common cold, the systems are the same. We have assimilated rape into our everyday culture much as we have the cold. Like the folklore surrounding the common cold, there is folklore about rape, like the notion that if a woman wears revealing clothing or goes to a bar alone, she is likely to "get raped." But in fact a woman is no more likely to be raped from these activities than from simply dating a man or being home alone.

There is a silence surrounding the recognition that we live

in a cultural environment where rape is endemic, but it is true. The rape culture is much like the poor sanitation conditions which led to typhoid—it provides an environment in which acts of rape are fostered. Look through any supposed women's publication and notice the ads that display women at the mercy of a man or at the mercy of the male gaze. Notice the articles that emphasize dependence and passivity and avoid portraying independence and strength in women. Watch TV shows that display precocious models of sexually manipulated teen-aged women. Walk into any bar and watch the women primp and the men pounce, and watch, too, as the number of unreported rapes turns into the number of women socialized into accepting this sort of sexual behavior as standard—not even recognizing rape when it occurs. Rape is part of the natural flora of our society and our world. . . .

Rape as Symptomatology

A study of the rape culture done by the University of California at Davis found: "the high incidence of rape in this country is a result of the power imbalance between men and women. Women are expected to assume a subordinate relationship to men. Consequently rape can be seen as a logical-extension of the typical interactions between men and women."

A disease is merely a set of symptoms combined into a neat medically identified package and labeled for public [consumption]. The germs are everywhere. The disease of rape is simply the set of symptoms of a socially oppressive system that allows men all the power and leaves women with all the shame. In fact, rape is quite pervasive and rigidly fixed into our social system. Everything from TV commercials for dish soap to the exchanges between men and women in supermarkets are symptoms of the rape culture. It is part of the natural flora, the way things are. Men are trained to rape and women to take it. Rape is taught and learned through these patterns and paradigms without the word rape ever being uttered. . . .

Unless we constantly struggle against social pressures, women are brainwashed into thinking that we HAVE to do certain things to be accepted. Women smile more than men, we take up less space, we defer to men as they interrupt our conversations, we apologize before stating an opinion, and we strive day in and day out to perfect our bodies for the male gaze. This is the rape culture. When men decide that they want, we give. When we say no, we apologize. Our no's are interrupted by their yes's. And we sexualize our bodies for the world of men and not for ourselves; therefore we don't love them enough to protect them. These small-seeming social actions translate into sexual assault as they reach the bedroom.

Young Women and the Rape Culture

Because of feminism's many successes, women have been seduced into submission once again. In the beginning of the 21st century, many more women than not are convinced that we have reached equality with men. This is a dangerous conviction, primarily because it is not true. The reason the rape culture is endemic to American women is because we have the illusion that we exist in a safe space, where rape only happens to women who jog late at night in Central Park. The term "date rape" is often mocked among my peers as a creation by sexually insecure women. And feminism is a dirty word, as those of us with vocal feminist views know all too well.

The advertisements and music videos depict women in skimpy clothing with beckoning looks on their faces.

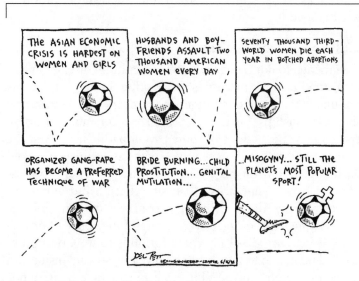

Pett. © 1998 *Lexington Herald-Leader*. Reprinted with permission.

Women with small and impossible bodies are what we aspire to because that is what men are attracted to. And women are first and foremost supposed to be attractive to men. But women, particularly women in college, are also told that we are smart, liberated, equal to men, and have some inner goddess—strength. These contradictory messages can be confusing and keep us enthralled by the rape culture if we let the belief that we have social equality blind us to the subliminal messages embedded in the media.

To be a young woman today means to live with the rape culture in all its subtleties. It means to act in accordance with the roles that keep men forever in power. I may be a smart, educated, self-confident woman of the modern day, but any man who wants to can rape me because he is stronger. Not only physically stronger, but psychologically stronger because he was taught by the system to be aggressive and take what he feels he deserves. To be a young woman often means to buy *Glamour* and *Vogue* and take the advice that pleases men. It means to fluctuate body weight to please the day's fashion archetype. Being a young woman today means to be unhappy if men don't like the way you look. I have cried many a night because of my big shoulders and my skinny, white legs, and I still struggle to find my own definition of what is sexy.

Cultural Cures for Rape

The media do not recognize rape as a cultural disease. When magazines or news programs do examine the subject, it is often under the guise of stranger rape or rape in severely abusive relationships. Or it is identified as a potentially passing epidemic or the actions of some psychopathic man. And the solution suggested by this same media is avoidance. Avoid dark streets (obviously), avoid bad situations (well, to most of us, a bar in general is a bad situation), avoid going out alone, walking alone, drinking too much, dressing too revealingly, being too aggressive, smiling too profusely, or acting too insecure. Basically the solution is to walk on tiptoes around men, and to take back the night by staying inside and watching a good movie. The solution to rape as it stands now is to let men continue to do this until women are too scared to leave their homes alone or in groups, or even to live alone because men hold the ultimate power of decision. Men hold in their big hands the power over women's sexual safety. That is simply not good enough.

Rape is endemic because it pervades every aspect of our complex social structure. In order to vaccinate against it, we would have to change many parts of society that people are fully comfortable with and accepting of. Patriarchy is still very much at work, only more subtly. There is a defiance of admitting weakness because weakness is devalued and to be raped in these flicked up days, is to be weak. Postmodern theory waxes on about inclusion and identity politics; liberals pretend equality has been achieved. And because of the code of sex-positive cool, young women accept these stances at face value and ignore the ongoing perpetuation of rape culture.

Rape is not an epidemic that spiked mysteriously in the mid-seventies when feminists called attention to it. It is not a sudden outbreak that can be cured with a single vaccine. It is an endemic social disease that pervades every walk of life imaginable. This is the rape culture—millions of small-seeming social germs translate into sexual assault as they reach the bedroom.

In rape-crisis training, I learned what makes men rape. And it is not some inbred sexual urge that is just part of man's biology. It is power and privilege. I learned what keeps women silent. It is fear. My experience with the rape culture wasn't the same as women who had the misfortune to be physically forced to have sex. But mine is frightening because I, like a zombie, played the cards I had been dealt and didn't even think about how seduced I was by the mainstream suggestions for male/female behaviors.

In my biology class I learned that small pox has been virtually eradicated and only exists in isolated labs. It used to be a rampant epidemic. If science can stamp out such a pervasive disease, and if a developing economy can get rid of typhoid, then an aware and educated society with new values can eliminate the social germs of rape. We can stop rape in this new century—if we are ready to identify the aspects of our cultural environment that foster rape and eliminate them.

"It is becoming increasingly apparent that the new style of warfare is often aimed specifically at women and is defined by a view of premeditated, organized sexual assault."

Rape Is Frequently Used as a Weapon of War

Barbara Crossette

In the following viewpoint, Barbara Crossette contends that wartime rape is no longer a random event but is increasingly used in conflicts to facilitate ethnic cleansing. According to Crossette, modern combatants see rape as a way to destroy minority cultures by humiliating their women, whose chastity is often central to cultural and religious beliefs. Moreover, she asserts, aggressors look at rape as a way to impregnate women with the majority group's children, thereby increasing the majority's dominance. Crossette also notes that the threat of rape is an effective method of forcing a population to flee from disputed territories. Barbara Crossette writes for the *New York Times*.

As you read, consider the following questions:
1. In what recent ethnic conflicts has rape been used to facilitate ethnic cleansing, according to Crossette?
2. How were women in Rwanda used to conduct genocide, as reported by the author?
3. As stated by Crossette, how do many women react to being raped during ethnic conflicts?

They strike without warning, bringing terror to an apartment in Algeria, a Chinese shop in Indonesia, a squalid refugee encampment in Africa or a Balkan farming village under siege. They are shadowy men with causes so blinding and hatreds so deep that they have transformed modern warfare into orgies of primordial savagery—raping, brutalizing, humiliating, slashing and hacking women and girls to death.

More civilians than soldiers are being maimed and killed in the wars of nationalism and ethnicity that are the hallmark of the twentieth century's end, wars fought in neighborhoods rather than battlefields.

More to the point, it is becoming increasingly apparent that the new style of warfare is often aimed specifically at women and is defined by a view of premeditated, organized sexual assault as a tactic in terrorizing and humiliating a civilian population. In some cases the violators express a motive that seems to have more in common with the tactics of ancient marauding hordes than with the twentieth century— achieving forced pregnancy and thus poisoning the womb of the enemy.

From Bosnia to Indonesia

International attention first focused on the use of rape as a tactic of warfare in Bosnia, where a United Nations commission and human rights groups found that ethnic Serb paramilitary groups had systematically tolerated or encouraged the raping of Bosnian Muslim women as part of the effort to drive Muslims from their homes and villages between 1991 and 1995.

Rape was also employed by Hutu troops against Tutsi women in the genocidal campaign Hutu leaders conducted in Rwanda in 1994. In 1997, women who have identified with secular culture in Algeria accused desperate rebels fighting in the name of Islamic revolution of kidnapping them and making them sex slaves. In Indonesia, reports are surfacing that suggest members of the security forces may have been among the men who raped ethnic Chinese women during rioting.

And in the Balkans, Serbs [began emptying] towns of a rival ethnic group—this time Albanians in Kosovo—and human rights and women's groups are monitoring the growing violence for the possibility that rape will again be one of the techniques.

None of this is the essentially random rape that traditionally follows conquest, intolerable though that is; it is different even from forcing conquered women to be prostitutes for the victors, as Japan did in Korea during World War II.

The difference is that in all four recent cases, sexual degradation and intimidation—often public—seem to have been used as a strategy of ethnic or religious conflict itself.

This use of rape as a premeditated act of warfare is challenging anew the efforts by nations of the world to organize effectively to prevent and punish crimes against humanity, a monumental task that moves into new territory [in June 1998] with the opening of a treaty conference in Rome to create the world's first international criminal court. Largely because of the systematic use of sexual assault in ethnic wars in the Balkans and Rwanda, the court is expected to rank rape as an internationally recognized war crime for the first time in history, alongside violence against noncombatants, mistreatment of prisoners, torture and other unusual punishments. [The court did agree to recognize rape as a war crime.]

The Rape Camps

Widney Brown, an advocate with the women's rights division of Human Rights Watch, echoed other experts when she said that rape "has probably been an issue in every major conflict, but what happened in Bosnia, particularly with the creation of the rape camps, really brought it to light." In the Balkans, where soldiers of every faction were accused of rape, the discovery of areas where Serbian soldiers confined Bosnian Muslim women to be raped shocked many. "In Yugoslavia rape was a part of ethnic cleansing, because the message that you got was if you stayed, the men would be murdered and the women would be raped," Ms. Brown said.

"That was followed very quickly by what happened in Rwanda, where we have similar widespread allegations of rape and mutilation," she added. "In fact, part of the preliminary campaign that created the atmosphere that allowed the genocide to happen was the demonization of Tutsi women as oversexualized creatures who were seductresses. It's not surprising that during the conflict they were subjected to rape, and a lot of sexual mutilation. Mutilation is another way of saying, 'We don't perceive of this person as a human being.'"

[Since about 1993], ad hoc tribunals have been hearing allegations of war crimes, first in the Balkans and later in Rwanda, and these tribunals have already decided to consider rape a war crime in those conflicts. Since they have been serving as small-scale models for the permanent international court that court is expected to follow suit.

Forced Pregnancy

The extent of sexual violence often becomes evident long after the world knows the extent of other crimes. Stories of sexual violence in Rwanda emerged approximately nine months after the genocide had ended, as women began bearing babies conceived as a result of rape. According to estimates of the Rwandan National Population Office, women who survived the genocide gave birth to between 2,000 and 5,000 children, who are often known as *"enfants des mauvais souvenirs"* (children of bad memories). The same pattern is true of the former Yugoslavia, where women were raped until they were pregnant and then held until they were close to term. In 1993, it was estimated that between 1,000 and 2,000 women became pregnant as a result of rape in the former Yugoslavia.

Valerie Oosterveld, *UNESCO Courier,* July/August 1998.

"These tribunals were literally forced to pay attention to a series of petitions and pressures from women's organizations demanding that rape be recognized," said Felice Gaer, an expert on human rights and international organizations for the American Jewish Committee. Ms. Gaer said that ultimately the support of Justice Richard Goldstone, the first war crimes prosecutor for the Balkans and Rwanda, succeeded in elevating sex crimes to the level of genocide and crimes against humanity. This was the first step taken by nations trying to tackle collectively this new scourge of war. But women are drawing up a longer list of gender-related crimes in wartime, and promise a battle to have them recognized by the International Criminal Court.

Ken Franzblau, who tracks the sexual exploitation of women for Equality Now, a New York–based organization that aids women in poor nations and immigrant women here, said rape is so widespread now because it is so effective in ethnic wars.

"It has such devastating effects on communities, particularly in traditional societies or very religious communities where the virginity and the fidelity of women can be central to the makeup of that society," he said. Rape is a psychological grenade thrown into the middle of daily life to provoke maximum terror. "That's why you see a fair number of these rapes committed in front of family members of the girls or women involved," he said.

Some analysts believe that the fast pace of international communications today may be a factor in the rapid recurrence of the use of rape as a tactic of war in such widely separate parts of the world. But if that is true, it is also evident that rapid international communication has played a role in stirring international outrage about the tactic.

In the 1990s, there have been significant changes among the vulnerable women themselves. Women who were the victims of sexual abuse in the name of ethnic purity, nationalism and sometimes religious zeal have begun to speak out, often aided by human rights organizations and women's crisis centers. For many, this has been a revolutionary change.

Beyond Suicide

"Lots of women just committed suicide in the past," said Charlotte Bunch, executive director of the Center for Women's Global Leadership at Rutgers. "That's one very clear thing that's beginning to emerge now. In the 1990s, the outrage that women have been able to raise about the issue means that people are reporting it. But the truth is that there is also a backlash about women speaking out. There may be some moments before we reach a point where there is enough outrage to get the phenomenon under control."

The phenomenon takes human form in a number of recent accounts reported by journalists. Take the story of Nawal Fathi, who was captured by militants in Algeria in 1996, made into a sex slave and raped by a score of men before being rescued by government troops. A psychiatrist who treated her said that despite a year of medical treatment, Ms. Fathi committed suicide at the age of 24.

In Jakarta, aid workers were quoted as saying that hundreds of ethnic Chinese women had been sexually assaulted during the looting of Chinese neighborhoods, apparently by organized gangs that may have had links to security forces. "Some of the attackers said, 'You must be raped because you are Chinese and non-Muslim,'" one woman recalled. Again, a number of women have killed themselves rather than live in shame.

Outside Religion

Although militants in Algeria and roving gangs of rapists in Indonesia are Muslims, the phenomenon is probably not related to religion, though radical religious views may provide justification to an elemental misogyny. The Taliban movement in Afghanistan, for example, has repressed women but its holy warriors have not abused them sexually, as their predecessors in the Mujahedeen armies were frequently accused of doing, Afghan women say. Roman Catholics butchered other Roman Catholics in Rwanda and Burundi. Sex slaves are also a hallmark of the vaguely evangelical Lord's Resistance Army in Uganda. Burmese troops in Myanmar, a Buddhist country, are accused from the human-rights group Earthrights of using rape as a weapon against women from 20 or more ethnic minorities or student groups that oppose the military regime.

Because women displaced by ethnic warfare or other forms of mass violence are often not safe even in refugee camps—or arrive there pregnant through rape—United Nations relief agencies and some private groups have begun to offer gynecological services and the "morning after" pill, which prevents conception. Although this practice has been sharply criticized by anti-abortion groups in the United States, the United Nations High Commissioner for Refugees, Sadako Ogata, and others have continued to provide help to abused women.

At Equality Now, Mr. Franzblau said the kind of sexual abuse that took place in Bosnia, where Serb rapes of Muslim women were numerous and intense personal hatred was directed at neighbors, not some distant stranger at an enemy gun emplacement, makes the impact much worse and stokes the fires for the next round of strife.

"That's why it is going to be very difficult to reconcile these communities," he said. "How can you move families back to homes where a mother or daughter or sister was raped by a next-door neighbor?"

"Sex offenders who prey on children go where children are."

Schools Often Contribute to Child Sexual Abuse

Economist

In the following viewpoint, the *Economist* claims that many institutions created to educate and nurture children in fact allow the sexual abuse of children to take place. The magazine asserts that school personnel such as teachers, bus drivers, and athletic coaches are much more likely than strangers are to molest children. Unfortunately, instead of reporting known sex offenders to the authorities, schools often quietly transfer them to other districts, where they usually strike again, according to the *Economist*. Lawsuits against such institutions for failing to report offenders may lead to less abuse, but in the meantime, the *Economist* suggests that institutions should conduct thorough background checks of all new hires and limit the time any adult spends alone with a child. The *Economist* is a newsmagazine.

As you read, consider the following questions:
1. As reported by the *Economist*, how did Mark Fry's high school deal with him after he was discovered on the roof of a student's house?
2. What percentage of child sexual abuse cases are attributed to "acquaintance molesters," as cited by the author?
3. According to the *Economist*, how should parents protect their children from acquaintance molesters?

The Catholic church is not the only institution that needs to confront, and deal with, sexual crimes against children.

Some time around midnight on August 19th, 1991, Mark Fry, a high-school history teacher in a wealthy Chicago suburb, was arrested on a student's roof. He was dressed in black, wearing a ski mask and carrying a can of Mace. School officials, fearful of bad publicity, did what many otherwise decent people do in such cases: they wrote glowing letters of recommendation for Mr Fry and sent him somewhere else. He became a high-school principal in Wisconsin, where he was arrested and convicted seven years later for molesting a student.

Illuminating Abuse's Dark Corners

As the Roman Catholic church squirms in the spotlight over charges of sexual abuse of young people, that spotlight needs to be shone in some other corners. Sex offenders who prey on children go where children are, says Ernie Allen, president of the National Centre for Missing and Exploited Children. They teach in schools, coach sports teams, run scout troops and day-care centres. Charol Shakeshaft, a professor at Hofstra University and the author of a book on sexual violence in schools, has found that 15% of pupils are sexually abused by a teacher or staff member between kindergarten and high-school graduation, and that up to 5% of teachers sexually abuse or harass students. A recent FBI child-pornography sting, Operation Candyman, nabbed a teacher, a teacher's assistant, a school bus driver and an athletics coach.

On April 15th, 2002, Baruch Lanner, an Orthodox rabbi, went on trial in New Jersey for sexually abusing two teenage girls while he was the principal of a Jewish day school. Orthodox authorities stand accused of ignoring evidence that Rabbi Lanner sexually abused more than 20 teenage girls while he was in a position of authority in the Orthodox Union's National Conference of Synagogue Youth. In 1999, *Sports Illustrated* described American youth sports, in which millions of children are coached or supervised by unscreened male volunteers, as "a ready-made resource-pool for paedophiles".

Why is it so hard to protect children? To begin with, adults are often looking for predators in the wrong places.

Parents teach their children to fear strangers, yet abductions off the street are a small fraction of child sex-abuse cases. Counsellors and teachers are trained to recognise sexual abuse by family members. Yet a third group, so-called "acquaintance molesters," is responsible for about 40% of sexual abuse cases—and a higher percentage of crimes against boys.

The victims are often reluctant to come forward. Acquaintance molesters identify vulnerable children and shower them with attention, affection and gifts. The victim is left feeling complicit, and his guilt and shame make it unlikely that the crime will be reported. Studies of sex offenders in jail have found that the average child molester has gained legitimate access to children, begun molesting by the age of 15, and abused nearly 120 victims, most of whom never report the crime.

The Sexual Predator Coach

The sexual predator coach works hard at establishing athlete and parental trust, and frequently is a "charmer," making it unthinkable to most people that he would engage in this behavior. He often promotes himself by making promises regarding the star potential of children he coaches. He carefully structures the coaching environment so that there are opportunities to be alone with specific athletes during practice and road games. The acts are not random, but well-planned and aimed directly at athletes who either will do almost anything to get to the top of their field or are from broken homes. Sexually abusive coaches also know that, because of the athlete's desire to get a scholarship and/or make the team, it is unlikely that the abuse will be reported.

Leonard D. Zaichkowsky, *USA Today*, January 2000.

When an allegation is made, the victim is often a troubled or delinquent young person. The accused adult, however, may be a pillar of the community—in many cases, because of his eagerness to do extra work with children. Communities desperately seek to convince themselves that a particular sex offender is different because of his other good deeds. "Adult human beings tend to believe what they need to believe, and the stronger the need, the stronger the tendency," says Kenneth Lanning, a retired FBI behavioural analyst and an expert on the sexual victimisation of children. He points to a case in which 20 teachers testified in a trial on behalf of a convicted colleague, describing him—without irony—as a "child magnet".

By and large, as Ms Shakeshaft points out, institutions protect the adults and not the children. At worst, fearing legal liability and damage to their reputations (and often prodded by lawyers and insurance companies), they come to a private settlement with the offender. "The first instinct is to get them out of your organisation," says Mr Allen. As in the case of Mr Fry, the perpetrator is sent away with nothing but praise in the personnel file. Such cases are so common that educators have coined the term "passing the trash". A 1995 study of 225 cases in which pupils were sexually abused by teachers or other staff members found that in only 1% of the cases did the school-district superintendent attempt to revoke the culprit's teaching licence.

That may be changing, in large part because the cost of covering up is rising. As cases of abuse receive more publicity, parents and victims have begun to win lawsuits against schools that either fail to sack teachers with a history of sexual abuse or ship known offenders elsewhere. Still, an awful lot of trash is being passed around.

What Can Be Done?

What can be done? Any responsible institution ought to begin with a thorough background check of all potential volunteers or employees, checking their fingerprints against a national criminal database. Authorities should take note of seemingly innocuous past offences, Mr Lanning says, such as trespassing or disorderly conduct.

Second, every institution should have a system of management and supervision that limits the time any adult spends alone with a child. Listen to rumours, says Ms Shakeshaft. Although only 6–7% of victims report the abuse to someone in authority, most will tell their friends. "The kids tend to know," she says.

Lastly, a mechanism is needed to deal with allegations of abuse, some of which will turn out to be false. Any proven case must be prosecuted to the fullest, says Mr Allen. School administrators often believe that a tenured teacher cannot be removed if there is not sufficient evidence to build a criminal case. In fact, the standard of evidence is lower, and staff can be sacked even if the case cannot be prosecuted.

Above all, parents have to teach their children to be alert, and must take note of adults who cross the moral boundary. Let them remember that the problem of adults abusing positions of trust and authority by preying on young people is not confined to the Catholic church.

Periodical Bibliography

The following articles have been selected to supplement the diverse views presented in this chapter.

John P. Araujo — "Free Speech Should Not Cover Porn," *Texas Christian University Daily Skiff*, April 12, 2000.

Anita K. Blair — "Domestic Violence: Don't Always Assume the Man's to Blame," *Ex Femina*, April 2001.

Matthew Gever — "Pornography Helps Women, Society," *Daily Bruin*, December 3, 1998.

Erica Goode — "Human Nature: Born or Made? Evolutionary Theorists Provoke an Uproar," *New York Times*, March 14, 2000.

Neve Gordon — "Sanctioned Rape," *Humanist*, July 2000.

Jacky Hardy — "Everything Old Is New Again: The Use of Gender-Based Terrorism Against Women," *Minerva*, Summer 2001.

Owen D. Jones — "Law and the Biology of Rape: Reflections on Transitions," *Hastings Women's Law Journal*, Summer 2000.

Owen D. Jones — "Sex, Culture, and the Biology of Rape: Toward Explanation and Prevention," *California Law Review*, July 1999.

Alice Kim — "How Can We Put an End to Rape?" *Socialist Worker*, November 21, 1997.

Wendy McElroy — "Banning Pornography Endangers Women," International Society for Individual Liberty, 1997. www.seventhquest.net.

Ann E. Menashe — "An Interview with Diana Russell: Violence, Pornography, and Women Hating," *Against the Current*, July/August 1997.

Megan Rosenfeld — "The Male Animal: Two Scientists Explain Rape as a Natural Behavior and Cause an Uproar," *Washington Post*, January 28, 2000.

Lynn Segal — "Pornographic Battles," *Index on Censorship*, 2000.

Marianne Meed Ward — "An Equal-Opportunity Vice," *Alberta Report*, March 27, 2000.

Abigail Zuger — "A Fistful of Hostility Is Found in Women," *New York Times*, July 28, 1998.

Is Sexual Violence a Serious Problem?

Chapter Preface

Weeks after moving in with her new love, Maria discovered that the attentiveness she had been so flattered by was turning into obsessive jealousy. Her partner stalked her, imprisoned her in their home, kicked and punched her. One night at 3 A.M., Maria was caught trying to sneak from the home and was beaten and raped. After such episodes, Maria's partner would be contrite, even loving, but before long, the anger and jealousy would return, ultimately resulting in violence. Maria's story sounds distressingly familiar to anyone knowledgeable about domestic violence. However, Maria's case is unusual in one respect: Maria is a lesbian.

According to many experts, domestic violence between gays and lesbians is a common, if hidden, problem. While hate crimes against gays have been well publicized, violence within the gay community has not. A study by the National Coalition of Anti-Violence Programs reported 2,574 cases of domestic violence against lesbian, gay, bisexual, and transgendered individuals in 1998. According to Greg Merrill, coauthor of the coalition report, 25 to 33 percent of same-sex partners are victims of domestic violence, approximately the same percentage as found in heterosexual relationships. The study defined domestic violence as "verbal, physical, financial and/or sexual abuse occurring in the context of a romantic relationship."

Even though gay men, lesbians, and heterosexuals experience similar rates of domestic violence, many gay activists contend that abuse between gays and lesbians stems from different causes, such as internalized homophobia. According to Michael Bronski, a gay activist and author of *The Pleasure Principle: Sex, Backlash and the Struggle for Gay Freedom*, "Gay people are the only oppressed people born into the enemy camp. What does it mean that we are born into families where we understand that as soon as we know who we are, they hate us? They may love us as a son or daughter, but they would prefer us to be heterosexual. People are kept in line, and in the closet, by the threat of violence. And that threat follows us our entire lives." Bronski and others believe that such violence gets internalized and is acted out later against intimates.

In part because abuse within gay relationships does not fit neatly into existing domestic violence models, it has been difficult to address. One problem is that gays and lesbians are reluctant to report abuse and get help. According to Peter Sawires, coordinator of the Family Violence Prevention Fund's National Health Resource Center on Domestic Violence, "There's a tangible taboo against examining any kind of problem in gay and lesbian relationships, out of the real fear that someone like [evangelist] Jerry Falwell will grab on to it and distort it as another reason gay and lesbian relationships aren't healthy." Another reason gay domestic violence goes unreported is that gays and lesbians are afraid to acknowledge their homosexuality to authorities. There are institutional roadblocks as well. For example, many states have sodomy laws that would require a gay abuse victim to admit breaking the law in order to file an abuse claim. Another problem is that most shelters for victims of domestic violence are set up to protect heterosexual women, which leaves many gay abuse victims nowhere to go but the street.

In many ways, Maria was lucky. She did not wind up on the street—or worse, dead—because she had the support of friends and family. Many gay people, who are often rejected by their families, lack such a safety net. As studies on gay and lesbian domestic abuse show, sexual violence is more widespread than previously thought. The authors in the following chapter discuss other groups affected by sexual violence and debate the lasting effects of abuse on victims. Even though Maria was finally able to leave her abuser, she says, "Even now, sometimes I'm still afraid to walk the streets alone."

> "*The rape problem is big enough and has been demonstrated enough times in enough different groups that it is time to get on with the rest of the agenda.*"

Rape Is a Serious Problem

Mary P. Koss

In the following viewpoint, Mary P. Koss contends that recent studies have proven once and for all that rape is a serious problem. She argues that critics who continually question rape research are hampering efforts to effectively deal with the crisis. Koss believes efforts to address rape are also undermined by the latest trend of lumping rape and domestic violence statistics together, which essentially makes rape invisible. Mary P. Koss is professor of public health, family, and community medicine; psychiatry; and psychology in the College of Public Health at the University of Arizona.

As you read, consider the following questions:
1. What percentage of women have been raped, according to the U.S. Department of Justice?
2. How has the use of criminal justice models in rape research impacted the study of rape, in the author's view?
3. In Koss's opinion, why is it important to consider gender while studying rape?

The evidence of social change is all around us as I was reminded with this story told by Katie Dusenberry [supervisor for Pima County, Arizona, and state transportation board representative]. Two 4-year-old boys were playing in the yard. One said to the other, "I found a contraceptive device under the veranda." The other little boy said, "Really. What's a veranda?"

Yes, things have changed. Yet, I resonate to writer Anna Quindlen's suspicions that, "Over the past twenty years, we've changed the world just enough to make it radically different, but not enough to make it work."

I first take my lead from the little boys and highlight how knowledge about rape has changed in the last five years in [the area of] rape prevalence. . . . Other significant areas where there is fascinating emerging knowledge that I won't have time to cover are cultural influences, medical impact, judicial processing, and broader societal costs of sexual assault. In the second half of my remarks, I'll focus on a critical analysis of the findings and consider some political implications for the anti-rape movement.

Rape Prevalence

Research on the scope of rape has been heavily criticized in the public media on many grounds. Striking close to home, Linda Seebach's 1999 editorial in the *Rocky Mountain News* following the release of the Colorado Department of Public Health & Environment and Colorado Coalition Against Sexual Assault Study carried the headline, "Sensationalized rape statistics not real picture." As I wrote in a letter to Seebach's editor, she did not do her homework. Colorado's findings belong in a context of several recent national surveys, and when viewed against that background, they are typical, not sensational.

• *Violence Against Women Survey*—A telephone survey of a nationally representative sample of 8,000 women and men funded by the U.S. Department of Justice reported rape prevalence of 17.6% among women when completed and attempted rape were added together, as is typically done in crime statistics. The rate for completed rape alone was 14.8%. The authors noted ethnic differences in the risk of rape, found that slightly more than half of first-time rape victims were less than 18 years old, and observed that 76% of women who were raped and/or physically assaulted after age 18 were attacked by a current or former husband, co-habiting partner, or date. These findings reaffirm earlier findings well-known in the anti-rape movement, and importantly, also attach the cachet of federal sponsorship to them.

• *The National College Health Risk Behavior Survey*—A nationally representative survey of 4,838 college students funded by the Centers for Disease Control and Prevention reported a rape prevalence of 20% for college women recalling their entire lifetime and 15% since age 15. This figure is virtually identical to that reported by Koss, Gidycz, & Wisniewski in the first national survey of college students completed in 1985. The data also confirmed links of victimization and risky health behaviors including drinking, smoking, drug use, lack of condom use, overweight, and low physical activity level.

• *The U.S. Naval Recruit Health Study*—A national sample of 3,776 male and female recruits filled out questionnaires at the beginning of basic training. Of women recruits, 36% had been raped and 1% of the men reported perpetrating such acts prior to military service. These data are significant because they address concerns that college student samples may be oversensitive to issues of victimization thereby creating inflated estimates of rape. The naval recruits represent an ethnically and economically diverse sample of youth not attending college. Female sailors' rates of victimization are 2.4 times higher than college women and male sailors' rates of perpetration are 3.3 times higher than reported by college men.

• *Crime in the Ivory Tower*—This nationally representative sample of 3,472 college students were administered the National Crime Victimization Survey (NCVS) crime incident screening questions, including the measurement of rape that has been severely criticized even by scholars within the field of criminology. The reported rate of rape was 4% off campus and 4.3% on campus when the prevalence period was limited to the last 6–9 months. These figures are lower than the previous results because the screening questions used have been criticized as vague and ambiguous and the reference period was far shorter than standard practice in the field. Yet even these low figures were over three times higher than the NCVS reports for the nation. The authors attribute the discrepancy to the likelihood that the risk of sexual assault is higher on campus than in the general community. This may be true, although the Navy results suggest that college students are not the highest risk group of young Americans. More likely is that the insensitivity of the NCVS questions led to underidentification of rape here as they do in the parent study.

• *Behavioral Risk Factor Survey*—Sexual assault module, Colorado, 1999. This survey was administered to 1,802 Coloradans. Results revealed a 14% prevalence rate for completed rape among women and 2% among men. This rate is virtually identical to the national rate reported for completed rape in the National Violence Against Women (NVAW) Survey (14.8% women, 2.1% men).

You can see from review of these studies that through the accumulation and convergence of findings, the field has outgrown criticisms that the data are inconsistent, that national scope is lacking, and that the samples are unrepresentative or tapping respondents uniquely vulnerable to rape. . . .

Playing the Numbers Game

• *Prevalence numbers have converged.* The figures presented earlier demonstrate that prevalence estimates have converged. I think we know enough about how to contextualize a survey and frame the questions to identify rape, the kinds of methodological choices that suppress identification of rape, and the levels of rape one can expect to find based in the convergence of existing data. With the single exception of poor data on rape prevalence among ethnic groups, assertions that we don't have good data or that we need to devote resources toward the ultimate epidemiological study I now interpret in political terms. There is no such thing as objective science. Human values inevitably enter into defining the phenomena of interest, determining the appropriate sample, making scoring rules to include and exclude certain acts, and selecting the method of data collection. I am tired of playing the numbers game. It's a way to get a lot of activity, to get

When Is Rape Okay?

During a poll of high school students, Jacqueline Goodchilds asked the following question: "Is it all right if a male holds a female down and physically forces her to have sex if . . ."

Conditions	Percentage of "yes" responses	
	Males	Females
He spent a lot of money on her?	39%	12%
He is so turned on he thinks he can't stop?	36%	21%
She has had sexual intercourse with other guys?	39%	18%
She is stoned or drunk?	39%	18%
She lets him touch her above the waist?	39%	28%
She is going to and then changes her mind?	54%	31%
She has led him on?	54%	26%
She gets him excited sexually?	51%	42%
They have dated for a long time?	43%	32%

Jacqueline Goodchilds, www.fearus.org.

factions debating with each other, and a way to spend a lot of money.

• *Internal fighting at justice.* Evidence for this assertion might be the current bickering that is occurring between two bureaus of the U.S. Department of Justice over the National Violence Against Women Survey and why its numbers indicate a much larger rape problem than that identified by another justice survey, the National Crime Victimization Study. The loser is the American public, which continues to receive no clear awareness of the problem of rape from these authoritative sources. The rape problem is big enough and has been demonstrated enough times in enough different groups that it is time to get on with the rest of the agenda.

• *Has prevalence become a way to resist change?* Obstacles to action don't lie in deficient science or lack of data, they lie in resistance to change.

Decontextualizing Rape

Rape is being decontextualized in several different ways.

• *Lumping rape and domestic violence.* Activists and academics from both the rape movement and the domestic violence movement lobbied Congress to increase funds for research and services through legislation titled the Violence against Women Act. Everyone agrees that rape is a form of violence against women. But, in the implementation of the Act's initiatives rape has become a form of domestic violence. The effect of this labeling change is to make rape become invisible. At recent regional meetings, representatives from the Centers for Disease Control and Prevention have showed up wearing tee shirts with the slogan ". . . and sexual assault," to demonstrate their concerns that rape is being treated as an add-on. The practical implication of sweeping rape into domestic violence is that the planning and implementation of the Violence against Women Act initiatives have been dominated by people whose experience is with women fleeing abusive husbands. There is empirical evidence that when rape is treated in the context of domestic violence that it receives fewer resources than when freestanding. I fear that this conceptual practice coupled with the trend towards deradicalization in the advocate community, raises realistic fears that rape research and services will claim a decreasing share of available resources.

• *Imposition of criminal justice models.* Because rape is a crime, the Violence against Women Office was placed in the Justice Department and the National Institute of Justice has assumed the lead role in carrying out the initiatives of the Violence against Women Act. An unintended consequence of these decisions is that conceptual models applied to rape have become increasingly informed by criminology and public health. Each have different ways to label and think about rape as a phenomenon. Rape is neither an impersonal street crime, nor is it a disease. The following are two examples of problems that arise from the application of criminal justice models.

a) *Nonsensical analysis of trends in rape.* The tendency of criminologists to analyze rape trends along with other crimes is misleading. Rape is primarily an acquaintance phenomenon, is very inadequately captured in crime statistics due to underreporting, has identified causal factors that are completely different from those linked with other crimes, and it is unlikely to be affected by the predictors of most crimes such as community policing programs or number of people incarcerated. Lastly, there is no reason to expect that levels of rape would change over short time intervals, given the tenacity of the fundamental gender constructs that drive it.

b) *Gangs and guns school violence prevention.* The results of middle and high school student surveys reveal very high levels of psychological, physical, and sexual abuse of peers. Yet, review of the voluminous reviews, studies, and programs for school and community developed under aegis of the justice department reveals no acknowledgement that the problem of school violence is bigger than gangs and guns, nor is there acknowledgement that the number of persons affected by these intimate forms of violence is far larger than other expressions of youth violence.

The advocacy community needs to think about and counteract the criminological conceptual view of rape.

• *Lack of gender analysis.* I refer to the trend to analyze rape outside of the context of a gender analysis.

a) *Degendering of school violence.* Not only do dominant criminological models ignore intimate violence, they also do not support a gender analysis of school violence. Yet, one needs only look at the photos of the 11 mass shooters since 1997, including the six who were teenagers, to see the connection of violence and sex. The U.S. does not have a youth violence problem, we have a boy violence problem. We do not have a mass murder problem, we have a male killer problem. That gender-related violence and gender issues aren't being targeted in public policy illustrates how the operating conceptual scheme is creating large blind spots.

b) *PTSD model of trauma response.* The trauma research community also decontextualizes rape. It is just one of a number of interchangeable . . . phenomena that can trigger symptoms of post traumatic stress disorder (PTSD). The result is that our research literature is dominated by studies in which the impact of rape is only assessed from the perspective of PTSD symptoms. The result is an incomplete capture of the ways in which rape creates harm. Rape is unique because of its historical link to irremediable harm, the influence of gender and culture on lay views of what causes rape, and the influence of these factors on the recovery environment a rape survivor faces. Scholars and advocates need to keep their focus on the unique issues raised by rape even as we form coalitions to further scientific and political agendas.

c) *"Rape" of men.* Another example of a lack of gender analysis is the flow of research seeking to measure the sexual victimization of men by women and trying to write sexual victimization screening questions that are "sex neutral." From this perspective, a man can be raped if he voluntarily inserted his penis in a woman but felt she psychologically coerced him to do so. No one wants to downplay the rape of men by other men, which in my experience represents some of the most horrible victimizations I have ever worked with. This line of work not only trivializes male rape, but inevitably leads to less empathy for women rape victims, a level of concern that is not currently so high that we can afford to lose ground.

d) *Anti-victim sentiments.* Many younger women reject the term feminism, considering it the new "F" word. They endorse instead deeply held beliefs that they are strong and equal to men, have equal opportunity to do anything they want. That young women view themselves in these ways is very positive and representative of the accomplishments women in previous generations have made within the feminist movement. However, such worldviews represent not only a repudiation of a gender context in which to view the relationships of men and women, but incomplete life experience, and lack of acknowledgement of the empirical evidence. The data clearly suggest that on average men are stronger than women and have access to more social power. From the perspective of proud and strong young women, subjects like rape, which primarily target women, are a threat to their worldview. There are only two solutions to such a conflict. The first is to change your worldview to encompass the evidence. However, this solution is rendered less likely by the well-known human resistance to change. The remaining strategy is to deny that rape is really a problem. This strategy propelled Katie Roiphe [who was then a doctoral candidate in English at Princeton University] to her 15 minutes of fame by denying the rape problem on the Princeton University campus. The denigration of the term "victim" and the backlash against a "victim mentality" by women can be seen as a defense against the powerlessness and second class status they would feel if the reality of rape were acknowledged. As advocates and avowed feminists, we need to think about how the lack or repudiation of gender analysis is hindering communication of our message and think creatively about new language that preserves the ideas without the baggage. . . .

Our Work Is Not Done

The last decade of the 20th century will be remembered among other advances for its flurry of policy initiatives directed at violence against women. I have reviewed some of the exciting advances in the understanding of rape that have been accomplished in the closing years of the 20th century. But as [author] Irene Peter reminds us, "Just because everything is different doesn't mean anything has changed." I have shared some of my fears about how conceptual models, funding initiatives, and methodological disputes can tie up energy and waste resources. These observations are the basis of my fear that the first 10 years of the 21st century will fail to duplicate the progress made in the last years of the old one. I am convinced that the rape agencies have articulated our mission the best. We have to collaborate and be inclusive and at the same time have our own values and well-articulated agenda always at the ready. My message is, "Our work is not done."

> "[There is a] tremendous gap between
> estimates of rape . . . that emerge from
> data collected annually by the Bureau of
> Justice Statistics and the figures reported
> in advocacy studies."

The Prevalence of Rape Has Been Exaggerated

Neil Gilbert

Neil Gilbert argues in the following viewpoint that many feminists have exaggerated the incidence of rape by publishing advocacy research studies. According to Gilbert, such studies make the problem of rape seem larger than it really is by measuring the problem so broadly that many non-rape incidents are reported as rape. He contends that rape is indeed a serious problem but believes that advocacy research trivializes it and results in strained relations between men and women. Neil Gilbert is Chernin Professor of Social Welfare and Social Services at the School of Social Welfare of the University of California at Berkeley.

As you read, consider the following questions:
1. According to Koss's study, what percentage of women have been raped?
2. How do the authors of advocacy research studies make a problem such as rape appear larger than it really is, in the author's view?
3. In Gilbert's opinion, how do advocacy research studies on rape damage the relations between men and women?

According to the alarming accounts of sexual assault by certain feminist groups, about one out of every two women will be a victim of rape or attempted rape an average of twice in her life, one-third will have been sexually abused as children, and many more will suffer other forms of sexual molestation. These claims are based on figures from several studies, among which the *Ms.* Magazine Campus Project on Sexual Assault, directed by Mary Koss, . . . [is among] the most extensive, most widely disseminated, and most frequently cited.

[The study was] funded by the National Institute of Mental Health, giving [it] the imprimatur of endorsement by a respected federal agency. Often quoted in newspapers and journals, on television, and during the 1991 Senate hearings on sexual assault, the findings from [this study have] gained a certain degree of authority by process of repetition. Most of the time, however, those who cite the research findings take them at face value without an understanding of where the numbers come from or what they represent.

Serious Flaws

Prefaced by sophisticated discussions of the intricate research methods employed, the findings are presented in a blizzard of data, supported by a few convincing cases and numerous references to lesser known studies. But footnotes do not a scholar make, and the value of quantitative findings depends upon how accurately the research variables are measured, how well the sample is drawn, and the analysis of the data. Despite the respected funding source, frequent media acknowledgement, and an aura of scientific respectability, a close examination of [this] prominent [study] on rape reveals serious flaws that cast grave doubt on [its] credibility.

The *Ms.* study directed by Koss surveyed 6159 students at thirty-two colleges. As Koss operationally defines the problem, 27 percent of the female college students in her study had been victims of rape (15 percent) or attempted rape (12 percent) an average of two times between the ages of fourteen and twenty-one. Using the same survey questions, which she claims represent a strict legal description of the crime, Koss calculates that during a twelve-month period

16.6 percent of all college women were victims of rape or attempted rape and that more than one-half of these victims were assaulted twice. If victimization continued at this annual rate over four years, one would expect well over half of all college women to suffer an incident of rape or attempted rape during that period, and more than one-quarter of them to be victimized twice.

There are several reasons for serious researchers to question the magnitude of sexual assault conveyed by the *Ms.* findings. To begin with, a notable discrepancy exists between Koss's definition of rape and the way most women she labeled as victims interpreted their experiences. When asked directly, 73 percent of the students whom Koss categorized as victims of rape did not think that they had been raped. This discrepancy is underscored by the subsequent behavior of a high proportion of identified victims, 42 percent of whom had sex again with the man who supposedly raped them. Of those categorized as victims of attempted rape, 35 percent later had sex with their purported offender.

Problems with Definitions

Rape and attempted rape were operationally defined in the *Ms.* study by five questions, three of which referred to the threat or use of "some degree of physical force." The other two questions, however, asked: "Have you had a man attempt sexual intercourse (get on top of you, attempt to insert his penis) when you didn't want to by giving you alcohol or drugs, but intercourse did not occur? Have you had sexual intercourse when you didn't want to because a man gave you alcohol or drugs?" Forty-four percent of all the women identified as victims of rape and attempted rape in the previous year were so labeled because they responded positively to these awkward and vaguely worded questions. What does having sex "because" a man gives you drugs or alcohol signify? A positive response does not indicate whether duress, intoxication, force, or the threat of force were present; whether the woman's judgment or control were substantially impaired; or whether the man purposely got the woman drunk to prevent her from resisting his sexual advances. It could mean that a woman was trading sex for drugs or that a few drinks lowered the respondent's inhibitions and she consented to an act she later regretted. Koss assumes that a positive answer signifies the respondent engaged in sexual intercourse against her will because she was intoxicated to the point of being unable to deny consent (and that the man had administered the alcohol for this purpose). While the item could have been clearly worded to denote "intentional incapacitation of the victim," as the question stands it would require a mind reader to detect whether an affirmative response corresponds to a legal definition of rape.

Finally, a vast disparity exists between the *Ms.* study findings and the rates of rape and attempted rape that come to the attention of various authorities on college campuses. The number of rapes formally reported to the police on major college campuses is remarkably low—two-to-five incidents a year in schools with thousands of women. It is generally agreed that many rape victims do not report their ordeal because of the embarrassment and frequently callous treatment at the hands of the police. Over the last decade, however, rape crisis counselling and supportive services have been established on most major campuses. Highly sensitive to the social and psychological violations of rape, these services offer a sympathetic environment in which victims may obtain assistance without having to make an official report to the police. While these services usually minister to more victims than report to the local police, the numbers remain conspicuously low compared to the incidence of rape and attempted rape on college campuses as Koss defines the problem.

Applying Koss's finding of an annual incidence rate of 166 in 1000 women (each victimized an average of 1.5 times) to the population of 14,000 female students at the University of California at Berkeley in 1990, for example, one would expect about 2000 women to have experienced 3000 rapes or attempted rapes in that year. On the Berkeley campus, two rapes were reported to the police in 1990, and between forty and eighty students sought assistance from the campus rape counselling service. While this represents a serious problem, its dimensions (three to six cases in 1000) are a fraction of those (166 cases in 1000) claimed by the *Ms.* study. . . .

Advocacy Research

The *Ms.* study by Koss [is a] highly sophisticated example of advocacy research. Elaborate research methods are employed under the guise of social science, to persuade the public and policy-makers that a problem is vastly larger than commonly recognized. This is done in several ways: 1) by measuring a problem so broadly that it forms a vessel into which almost any human difficulty can be poured; 2) by measuring a group highly impacted with the problem and then projecting the findings to society-at-large; 3) by asserting that a variety of smaller studies and reports with different problem definitions, methodologies of diverse quality, and varying results, form a cumulative block of evidence in support of current findings; and 4) by a combination of the above.

Campus Date Rape Is Poppycock

[According to Camille Paglia] the pain of women who have suffered sexual assaults is diminished by lumping unwanted campus sex into the same category as violent attacks on women.

"Violence is the key," she said. "All along there has been this appalling callousness to the barbarism of stranger rape. Of all the campus cases that I have any knowledge of at all, 9 out of 10 are poppycock."

She said white, middle-class women project "this wide-eyed 'I'm just this little girl, won't you guide me?' The majority of time the guys are correctly reading the signals."

Nancy E. Roman, *Washington Times*, June 16, 1994.

Advocacy research is a phenomenon not unique to feminist studies of rape. It is practiced in a wide variety of substantive problem areas and supported by groups that, as [professor] Peter Rossi suggests, share an "ideological imperative," which maintains that findings politically acceptable to the advocacy community are more important than the quality of research from which they are derived. Playing fast and loose with the facts is justifiable in the service of a noble cause, just as is condemning or ignoring data and sentiments that challenge conventional wisdom. Denounced for expressing objectionable sentiments, for example, folk singer

Holly Dunn's hit, "Maybe I Mean Yes—When I Say No" was clearly out of tune with the feminist mantra, "no means no." The controversy over these lyrics ignored Charlene L. Muehlenhard and Lisa Hollabaugh's inconvenient findings that 39 percent of the 610 college women they surveyed admitted to having said no to sexual advances when they really meant yes and fully intended to have their way.

Although advocacy studies do little to elevate the standards of social science research, they sometimes serve a useful purpose in bringing grave problems to public attention. No matter how it is measured, rape is a serious problem that creates an immense amount of human suffering. One might say that even if the rape research magnifies this problem in order to raise public consciousness, it is being done for a good cause, and in any case the difference is only a matter of degree. So why make an issue of the numbers?

Bureau of Justice Statistics

The issue is not that advocacy studies simply overstate the incidence of legally defined rape, but the extent to which this occurs and what it means. After all, the difference between boiling and freezing is "only a matter of degree." The tremendous gap between estimates of rape and attempted rape that emerge from data collected annually by the Bureau of Justice Statistics (BJS) and the figures reported in advocacy studies have a critical bearing on our understanding of the issue at stake.

The BJS surveys, actually conducted by the Census Bureau, interview a random sample of about 62,000 households every six months. The confidentiality of responses is protected by federal law and response rates amount to 96 percent of eligible units. The interview schedule asks a series of screening questions such as: Did anyone threaten to beat you up or threaten you with a knife, gun or some other weapon? Did anyone try to attack you in some other way? Did you call the police to report something that happened to you that you thought was a crime? Did anything happen to you which you thought was a crime, but you did not report to the police?

A positive response to any of these screening items is followed up with questions like: What actually happened? How were you threatened? How did the offender attack you? What injuries did you suffer? When, where did it happen, what did you do, and so forth.

As a guide to trends in sexual assault, the BJS data show that rates of rape and attempted rape declined by about 30 percent between 1978 and 1988. As for recent experience, BJS findings reveal that 1.2 women in 1000 over twelve years of age were victims of rape or attempted rape. This amounted to approximately 135,000 female victims in 1989. No trivial number, this annual figure translates into a lifetime prevalence of roughly 5 to 7 percent, which suggests that one woman out of fourteen is likely to experience rape or attempted rape sometime in her life. As do other victimization surveys, the BJS studies have problems of subject recall, definition, and measurement, which, as Koss and others have pointed out, lead to underestimation of the amount of sexual assault.

Assuming that the BJS survey underestimated the problem by 50 percent—that is, that it missed one out of every two cases of rape or attempted rape in the sample—the lifetime prevalence rate would rise to approximately 10 to 14 percent. Although an enormous level of sexual assault, at that rate the BJS estimates would still be dwarfed by the findings of Koss, . . . which suggest that one in two women will be victimized an average of twice in their life.

All Men Are Rapists?

This brings us to the crux of the issue, that is, the huge differences between federal estimates and advocacy research findings have implications that go beyond matters of degree in measuring the size of the problem. If almost half of all women will suffer an average of two incidents of rape or attempted rape sometime in their lives, one is ineluctably driven to conclude that most men are rapists. "The truth that must be faced," according to researcher Diana Russell, "is that this culture's notion of masculinity—particularly as it is applied to male sexuality—predisposes men to violence, to rape, to sexually harass, and to sexually abuse children."

In a similar vein, Koss claims that her findings support the view that sexual violence against women "rests squarely in the middle of what our culture defines as 'normal' interaction between men and women." Catherine MacKinnon, one of the leading feminists in the rape crisis movement, offers a vivid rendition of the theme that rape is a social disease afflicting most men. Writing in the *New York Times* (December 15, 1991), she advises that when men charged with the crime of rape come to trial, the court should ask "did this member of a group sexually trained to woman-hating aggression commit this particular act of woman-hating sexual aggression?"

Advocacy research not only promulgates the idea that most men are rapists, it provides a form of "scientific" legitimacy for promoting social programs and individual behaviors that act on this idea. When asked if college women should view every man they see as a potential rapist, a spokeswoman for the student health services at the University of California, Berkeley told the *Oakland Tribune* (May 30, 1991), "I'm not sure that would be a negative thing." This echoes the instruction supplied in one of the most popular college guidebooks on how to prevent acquaintance rape. "Since you can't tell who has the potential for rape by simply looking," the manual warns, "be on your guard with every man."

Overreactions

These experts on date rape advise college women to take their own cars on dates or to have a back-up network of friends ready to pick them up, to stay sober, to go only to public places, to be assertive, to inform the man in advance what the sexual limits will be that evening, and to prepare for the worst by taking a course in self-defense beforehand. Separately, some of the instructions, such as staying sober, are certainly well advised. Collectively, however, this bundle of cautions transmits the unspoken message that dating men is a very dangerous undertaking.

Beyond seeking courses in self-defense, the implications drawn from advocacy research sometimes recommend more extreme measures. At a public lecture on "The Epidemic of Sexual Violence Against Women," Diana Russell was asked by a member of her largely feminist audience whether, in light of the ever-present danger, women should start carrying guns to protect themselves against men. Stating that personal armament was a good idea, but that women should probably take lessons to learn how to hit their target, Russell's response was greeted with loud applause.

Not all feminists, or members of the rape crisis movement, agree with the view that all men are predisposed to be rapists. Gillian Greensite, founder of the Rape Prevention Education program at the University of California, Santa Cruz, writes that the seriousness of this crime "is being undermined by the growing tendency of some feminists to label all heterosexual miscommunication and insensitivity as acquaintance rape." (One is reminded that 50 percent of the students whom Koss defined as victims of rape labelled their experience as "miscommunication.") This tendency, Greensite observes, "is already creating a climate of fear on campuses, straining relations between males and females."

Bad Studies Trivialize Rape

Heightened confusion and strained relations between men and women are not the only dysfunctional consequences of advocacy research that inflates the incidence of rape to a level that indicts most men. According to Koss's data, rape is an act that most educated women do not recognize as such when it has happened to them, and after which almost half of the victims go back for more. To characterize this type of sexual encounter as rape trivializes the trauma and pain suffered by the many women who are true victims of this crime, and may ultimately make it more difficult to convict their assailants. By exaggerating the statistics on rape, advocacy research conveys an interpretation of the problem that advances neither mutual respect between the sexes nor reasonable dialogue about assaultive sexual behavior.

It is difficult to criticize advocacy research without giving the impression of caring less about the problem than those engaged in magnifying its size. But one may be deeply concerned about the problem of rape and still wish to see a fair and objective analysis of its dimensions. Advocacy studies have, in their fashion, rung the alarm. Before the rush to arms, a more precise reading of the data is required to draw an accurate bead on this problem and attack it successfully.

"To the extent that society continues to deny the magnitude of childhood sexual abuse, it continues to behave irresponsibly in the matter of child molestation."

Child Sexual Abuse Is a Serious Problem

Rebecca M. Bolen and Maria Scannapieco

In the following viewpoint, Rebecca M. Bolen and Maria Scannapieco argue that the incidence of child sexual abuse, especially among girls, is disturbingly high. After conducting a thorough review of existing studies on child sexual abuse, the authors conclude that 30 to 40 percent of girls and 13 percent of boys are sexually abused. Unfortunately, according to the authors, only about one-quarter of children who are sexually abused are identified, assessed, and treated. Rebecca M. Bolen is assistant professor in the School of Social Work at Boston University. Maria Scannapieco is associate professor and director of the Center for Child Welfare, School of Social Work, University of Texas at Arlington.

As you read, consider the following questions:
1. In the authors' view, what institutions are impacted by estimates of the prevalence of child sexual abuse?
2. What factors contributed to the variability in prevalence estimates, according to Bolen and Scannapieco?
3. What percentage of cases of female child sexual abuse is being investigated and substantiated, as stated by the authors?

Rebecca M. Bolen and Maria Scannapieco, "Prevalence of Child Sexual Abuse: A Corrective Metanalysis," *Social Service Review*, vol. 73, September 1999, p. 281. Copyright © 1999 by *Social Service Review*. Reproduced by permission of the publisher and the author.

The study of the magnitude of childhood sexual abuse in our society has engaged many scholars through the years. Yet there is no agreement on the prevalence of sexual abuse in North America, despite the fact that establishing a reliable prevalence estimate has far-reaching implications for practice and policy in, but certainly not limited to, child welfare, mental health, law enforcement, and the medical profession. With estimates of the prevalence of child sexual abuse ranging from 2 percent to 62 percent, a great deal of misunderstanding and controversy exist.

Establishing a more reliable estimate of sexual abuse prevalence will influence and inform policy decisions made to address this social problem. Most of the reviews of prevalence studies point out various methodological concerns as the reason for the disparity in prevalence findings. However, only one empirical attempt has been made to evaluate the effects of these methodological concerns on sexual abuse prevalence. . . .

Literature Review

In this literature review, we describe and critique the methods of previous research reviews, explain how these methods affected their findings, and note how our review of prevalence studies will correct for their errors. Of the articles examined, we pay particular attention to the 1997 study of Kevin Gorey and Donald Leslie. . . .

For the purposes of this review, we included any article that reviewed sexual abuse prevalence studies. Many of these articles also included studies on the incidence of sexual abuse that are not considered here. We conducted an exhaustive review of peer-reviewed journals and books in an attempt to find all reviews of prevalence studies. We also searched multiple bibliographic databases such as Social Work Research and Abstract, ERIC, NISC Discover, PsychINFO, Sociological Abstracts, and Medline from 1980 through 1998, and we conducted manual searches of the more recent (1995–98) pertinent journals related to child maltreatment, such as *Child Abuse and Neglect, Child Maltreatment, Social Service Review, Social Work*, and *Child Welfare*. We included items in the review cohort if they (1) reported on sexual abuse prevalence studies, (2) were reports of research, and (3) were published in a professional journal or book. The search identified eight relevant articles for inclusion in this review's sample. . . .

Characteristics of the Studies

Only two of the eight research reviews restricted the reviews to population-based, randomized studies. College samples, community samples, and general population samples were reviewed in the majority of cases. Three of the eight research reviews included historical studies, and the other five included studies from 1979 to the present.

All but one review qualitatively compared the sexual abuse prevalence studies. Kevin Gorey and Donald Leslie's article was the first and only study to attempt to quantitatively analyze the extant body of research on the prevalence of child sexual abuse. Only one review limited study definitions of sexual abuse to contact only; all other research reviews included studies that examined noncontact as well as contact abuse, although two of the research reviews later adjusted the operational definition to contact only for summary estimates. Two research reviews included only studies that used random sampling, and one study included only females younger than 14 years of age. All research reviews included studies that examined both intrafamilial and extrafamilial sexual abuse.

Prevalence for females was estimated by half of the research reviews to be around 20 percent. Gorey and Leslie gave an unadjusted estimate of 22 percent for women, but when they adjusted for response rate they made a more conservative estimate of between 12 and 17 percent. This estimate is shared by William Feldman and colleagues, whose review concluded that prevalence has remained steady at about 12 percent and that "no increase in the prevalence of child sexual abuse of females younger than 14 years of age has occurred over the past four decades."

Four of the eight research reviews on prevalence of child sexual abuse reported on male estimates. All prevalence estimates for males were in the 5–10 percent range. Three of the eight research reviews did not attempt to estimate prevalence based on their review of the prevalence research.

Reviews by David Finkelhor as well as by Stephanie Peters and Gail Wyatt also concluded that the number of screening questions seemed to be the major source of variability among studies' prevalence estimates and that face-to-face interviews resulted in higher reporting. Timothy Wynkoop and colleagues also suggested that regional differences and problems with memory in retrospective surveys were causes for variability in prevalence.

Methodological Concerns

The methods of the research reviews varied greatly and may have affected the estimated prevalence. Feldman and colleagues estimated one of the lowest prevalences (12 percent) but considered only three research studies, one of which dated back to 1953. Another concern is that only two research reviews limited studies to only those using probability sampling. Including nonprobability samples reduces the generalizability of the findings and may impede the integration of findings across studies.

An examination of review methodologies reveals substantial differences, noted above, but also some similarities. The greatest similarity was that only one review used quantitative methods to compare studies. Gorey and Leslie's prevalence estimate was similar to that of other reviews until they quantitatively adjusted for response rate and thereby calculated a more conservative rate. . . .

The Present Study

Studies chosen for the current analysis had to use random sampling, and the population had to represent a community, state, or national North American adult population. To locate these studies, we used known studies and available reviews and searched PsychINFO and NISC Discover dating from 1980 to 1998 using "prevalence" and "child sexual abuse" as keywords. Because we had previously reviewed this literature, we were fairly certain that we had in our possession or knew of the majority of random prevalence studies. To verify this, however, we compared our list of studies with the reviews discussed previously. From these reviews, we eliminated studies of college samples or nonrandom samples. We eliminated other studies because they did not broadly define their populations or because they analyzed only intrafamilial abuse. We also removed studies that sampled only adolescents. During the course of our study we also heard about one additional study that had just been published. The data were reanalyzed after adding this latest study. . . .

The Implications of Our Findings

The current metanalysis moves the question of the prevalence of child sexual abuse for females in North America to a more substantial level. Through rigorous analysis and a review of the pertinent literature, we believe a reasonable estimate of the prevalence for female child sexual abuse is between 30 and 40 percent. For males, we believe that more than 13 percent have been sexually abused. Because the prevalence studies for males are so limited methodologically, we cannot at this time presume to know how many more have been abused. However, the *Los Angeles Times* Poll Survey, using only four screen questions, found that 16 percent of males were sexually abused in childhood. It is probably safe to say that at least this number of males have been sexually abused. These estimates of prevalence provide practitioners, policy makers, and researchers with a more reliable and valid estimation of the extent of this social problem.

By establishing an empirically based estimate of the prevalence of child sexual abuse, we expect and hope that the debate will move from minimizing this social problem to addressing its causes and treatment. To the extent that society continues to deny the magnitude of childhood sexual abuse, it continues to behave irresponsibly in the matter of child molestation. Additionally, with the awareness that childhood sexual abuse affects so many families and children, policy and practice can evolve to meet the needs of those affected by childhood sexual abuse. Removing the doubt that children are being victimized will reduce the overall trauma for the child and the family by providing the respect and professional response that is required.

To respond professionally to the magnitude of the problem, however, will require an overhaul of the existing child welfare system. In a National Incidence Study (NIS-3), 300,200 children were found to have been sexually abused during 1993, for an incidence rate of 4.5/1,000. The incidence rate for females was 6.8/1,000 and for males was 2.3/1,000. Even at the current levels of investigated and substantiated abuse, however, Andrea Sedlak and Diane Broadhurst state that "Child Protective Service (CPS) investigation has not kept up with the dramatic rise" in child maltreatment cases. Indeed, only 44 percent of all child sexual abuse cases in which harm occurred were investigated in 1993, down from 75 percent in 1986. Thus, the system cannot keep up even with the cases of which it is aware.

Looking in All the Wrong Places

Why is it so hard to protect children? To begin with, adults are often looking for predators in the wrong places. Parents teach their children to fear strangers, yet abductions off the street are a small fraction of child sex-abuse cases. Counsellors and teachers are trained to recognise sexual abuse by family members. Yet a third group, so-called "acquaintance molesters", is responsible for about 40% of sexual abuse cases—and a higher percentage of crimes against boys.

Economist, April 6, 2002.

Contrast this 6.8/1,000 incidence rate for females with projected incidence rates based upon prevalence estimates of 25 percent, 33 percent, and 40 percent. For example, for a 25 percent prevalence estimate, the concomitant incidence rate would be 25/1,000. Using the higher prevalence estimate of 40 percent, the concomitant incidence rate is 40/1,000.

Many Children Are Not Being Treated

Even with a prevalence of 25 percent, only 27 percent of incidents of female child sexual abuse are being investigated and substantiated by authorities. When the prevalence estimate increases to 33 percent, only 21 percent of cases are substantiated, decreasing to only 17 percent with a prevalence estimate of 40 percent. (We cannot calculate estimates for male child sexual abuse because we need the still unavailable average number of incidents of abuse for each victimized male.)

This analysis suggests that, even with the most optimistic

prevalence estimate, 73 percent of female children abused each year are not being identified, assessed, and treated. More realistically, up to 87 percent of female children are not being identified, assessed, and treated. While we cannot calculate similar projections for male children, it is probably safe to say that the majority are also not being properly identified. While some of this problem is the children's reluctance to disclose, it is also due in large part to the inability of the child welfare system to handle even the cases that come into the system. To intervene adequately, the child protective services system must expand substantially. Yet, the system as it currently exists cannot do so. The call must be for a complete overhaul of the system that allows for the potential for each abused child to be identified, assessed, and treated.

The Need for Better Studies

Another important implication for future research is that only the most rigorous prevalence studies will add to our current knowledge base. This review of studies has suggested that methodological variations affect the stated prevalence. With an issue of such importance, poorly designed studies will only contribute to confusion. Studies of prevalence should be methodologically rigorous or should not be done. The knowledge base as it now stands gives a fairly reliable, if somewhat broad, estimate for female child sexual abuse (30–40 percent). For female child sexual abuse, further research needs to narrow this range. For male sexual abuse, however, research needs to better define its prevalence, again using only the most methodologically rigorous studies.

The possibility that child sexual abuse continues to increase must also be considered. Researcher Diana Russell first suggested such a possibility when she examined cohort trends in her prevalence study. Given the findings and scope of the present study, research designed to better understand trends in child sexual abuse patterns and to consider societal patterns that may influence such patterns is necessary.

Perhaps the most important call for future research, however, is to move to the level of causality. Recently the General Accounting Office (GAO) concluded that "focuses on such topics as the causes and effects of child sexual abuse" and other topics are mostly irrelevant to "most local agencies' attempts to reform their services." Based upon findings of this review, we argue that research on the causes and effects of child sexual abuse is fundamental, not only to local agencies but also to state and federal agencies that provide funding and that legislate these agencies.

In a society in which 30 to 40 percent of all female children and 13 percent or more of male children are sexually abused, understanding causality is paramount for implementing appropriate prevention strategies. Given the prevalence of child sexual abuse, it is not enough to believe that child sexual abuse is, for example, simply a problem of family dysfunction. Instead, the role of the environment in which the child lives and especially the societal influences that allow for such propagation of tragedy must be opened to close scrutiny. Only when we understand the different pathways to abuse can we reduce the prevalence of abuse. Until then, we suggest that, for intervention efforts to be sufficient, federal and state governments must commit vastly increased resources to the problem of child sexual abuse.

"Child savers are those professionals who disseminate exaggerated claims of the prevalence of child sexual abuse in this country."

Some Professionals Exaggerate the Problem of Child Sexual Abuse

Thomas D. Oellerich

Thomas D. Oellerich maintains in the following viewpoint that some social workers are so concerned about protecting children that they exaggerate the dangers of child sexual abuse. According to Oellerich, many experts make erroneous claims about the existence of satanic rituals and repeat inaccurate statistics about the prevalence of child sexual abuse. Moreover, these professionals validate the most implausible claims about abuse and falsely argue that all forms of sexual activity involving minors are damaging to children. Thomas D. Oellerich is an associate professor in the Department of Social Work at Ohio University in Athens, Ohio.

As you read, consider the following questions:
1. What is a proselytizer, according to Oellerich?
2. As stated by the author, what is the actual prevalence of child sexual abuse?
3. How does the author define the "therapy marketeer"?

The recent allegations of sexual abuse in Wenatchee, Washington, suggest that the zealotry that marked such cases as the McMartin Preschool in Manhattan Beach, California, the Wee Care Day Care Center in New Jersey, the Little Rascals Day Care Center in North Carolina, and Faith Chapel in San Diego persists.[1] These cases represent a twentieth-century witch hunt. Child sexual abuse is immoral and illegal. Some children need protection. But, as indicated by these and other cases, they and their families need protection as well from [what R. Wexler calls] present day "child savers." These are the descendants of the child saving and child rescue movements of the nineteenth and early twentieth centuries. They are the professionals—social workers, therapists, physicians, law enforcement personnel, prosecutors—who, in their zeal to protect children, instead harm them and devastate the lives of families. . . .

A review of the literature suggests that child savers manifest certain beliefs concerning the problem of child sexual abuse. These beliefs, in turn, can serve as indicators for suspecting a professional may be a child saver.

The Proselytizer

The first indicator that a professional may be a child saver is when he or she becomes a *proselytizer*. This professional spreads the gospel of satanic ritual abuse, despite the absence of corroborative evidence for such allegations. K.V. Lanning (1991) reported that, despite intensive investigations over an eight-year period, law enforcement officials had found no credible evidence supporting allegations of ritual abuse. A five-year governmentally-funded study, conducted by G.S. Goodman, J. Qin, B.L. Bottoms, and P.R. Shaver (1994), concluded that hard evidence for satanic ritual abuse "was scant to nonexistent." And, more recently, B.L. Bottoms and S.L. Davis (1997) observed that there never were highly organized

1. In the early 1990s, twenty people were accused of sexually abusing children in Wenatchee, Washington; most of the accused were acquitted. In the 1980s, the McMartin preschool scandal resulted in over two-hundred counts of child molestation but not convictions. The Wee Care day care scandal, which occurred in the 1980s, resulted in the sentencing of Kelly Michaels to forty-seven years in prison for child sexual abuse. In 1992, a couple who ran the Little Rascals day care center was convicted of abusing twenty-nine children, but their convictions were overturned. The Faith Chapel scandal also involved allegations of child sexual abuse.

satanic ritual abuse cults in this country. They based this conclusion on their own surveys, the fact that the police and FBI agents have never found evidence of satanic ritual abuse, and the discrediting of and the recantations by alleged victims.

But the child savers firmly believe the claims of ritualistic abuse and continue to promulgate this notion. They reject reports as biased that do not corroborate the existence of satanic ritual abuse. The evidence, however, confirms the conclusion of the San Diego Grand Jury (1992, June), which investigated that county's child protective system and concluded that:

> the existence of satanic ritual abuse is a contemporary myth perpetuated by a small number of social workers, therapists, and law enforcement members who . . . cannot be dissuaded by a lack of physical evidence.

This contemporary myth is far from benign. As Bottoms and Davis (1997) point out, those who become involved with these professionals may live the rest of their lives with a false, painful belief. And they may act on this belief with untold harm to innocent individuals. These are often parents who are subjected to misguided lawsuits and imprisonment for crimes they did not commit.

The Validator

Second, child savers are those professional interveners who should remain objective but do not. They act as *validators* (Gardner, 1991). These professionals have as their purpose to "validate" even the most bizarre of allegations. The investigation of the Alicia Wade case by the San Diego Grand Jury (1992, June) revealed that county's child protective system to be inherently biased and unable to detect or correct its errors. In this system, social workers, therapists, investigators, and prosecutors operated on the presumption that an allegation of child sexual abuse meant that the abuse had in fact occurred. Evidence to the contrary was routinely ignored.

Indeed, the Grand Jury (1992, February) reported that some social workers may well have committed perjury in order to gain convictions. D. Lorandos (1995) also reports social workers withholding or falsifying information in civil proceedings in order to secure a judgment they deemed "in the best interests of the child."

The Exaggerator

Third, child savers are those professionals who disseminate exaggerated claims of the prevalence of child sexual abuse in this country. For example, they refer to the work of Diana Russell (1983) or Gail E. Wyatt (1985). Russell reported that more than half (54%) of all women experienced some form of intra- and extra-familial sexual abuse prior to age 18; Wyatt, that more than three-fifths (62%) of women had. As noted by P. Okami (1990), these prevalence rates far exceed the rates reported in virtually all other major studies.

These high rates, according to Okami, are the result of using moral and political criteria to define abuse. In this context, Okami points out that Russell's study was severely compromised by her selection and training of her interviewers. Moreover, both studies dismissed self-reports of inconsequential or of loving, noncoercive adult/nonadult sexual interactions as invalid interpretations of their experiences.

In point of fact, the actual prevalence of child sexual abuse is not known. Reports of prevalence from different surveys range from 6% to 62% for females and from 3% to 30% for males. Such a range of numbers hardly instills confidence about what is really known about the prevalence of child sexual abuse.

Estimates of the prevalence of child sexual abuse are complicated by variations in the definitions of sexual abuse, as E.E. Levitt and C.M. Pinnell (1995) note in their review of the literature. Definitions vary with respect to the types of behavior that is to be included, the age differences between those involved, and the presence or absence of coercion and/or force. Thus, some studies define sexual abuse as including everything from exhibitionism to rape to incestuous intercourse. Others use more narrow criteria. As a result, Levitt and Pinnell conclude that it is impossible to determine the true prevalence of child sexual abuse.

In a similar fashion, the child savers prefer referring to the numbers of *reported* cases of child sexual abuse. They ignore the fact that considerably less than half of reported cases are substantiated.

Additionally, child savers claim that the increased rate of reported cases reflects a real increase in prevalence. Thus, they assert there is an epidemic of child sexual abuse. But the evidence does not support this claim. W. Feldman, et al. (1991) compared data obtained in the 1970s and 1980s with data from the 1940s and found that the prevalence rates were similar. A.C. Kilpatrick (1992), in her study of 501 women from Florida and Georgia, found, when her data were analyzed by different age groups, a definite trend toward *decreasing* sexual activity among those 14 and under over the past 60 years, while the trend for adolescents had remained constant over that same period of time.

The child savers, however, prefer the larger numbers, as these provide them with what N. Gilbert (1991) refers to as "advocacy numbers" as opposed to legitimate numbers. Advocacy numbers are figures that are used to persuade public opinion that a problem is significantly greater than is generally recognized, rather than attempting to foster scientific understanding.

The Trauma Ideologist

Fourth, child savers are purveyors of what L.G. Schultz (1980) refers to as *trauma ideology*. Trauma ideologists regard every incident of sexual abuse as inevitably psychologically harmful, even devastating. That sexual contacts of a minor with an adult might be experienced without harm or even positively, is, to the child savers, heresy. For example, A.C. Kilpatrick (1992) concluded that early child and adolescent sexual experiences, unless there was force or high pressure involved, had no influence on later adult functioning regardless of the type of partner involved (i.e., relative or nonrelative) or the age differences. She reported that, when she discussed her findings with professionals, they closed their ears to them. They were most closed to those findings that indicated positive reactions to these early sexual experiences and to those findings that indicated that incestuous experiences did not cause irreparable harm.

The evidence suggests that, although child sexual abuse is *potentially* psychologically damaging, this is not always the case. A review of 45 studies by K.A. Kendall-Tackett, L.M. Williams, and D. Finkelhor (1993) concludes that up to 49% of the sexually abused children suffered no psychological harm. Thus, Kendall-Tackett, et al. concluded that a lack of symptoms could not be used to rule out sexual abuse since "there are too many sexually abused children who are apparently asymptomatic."

Among those with psychological harm, Kendall-Tackett, et al. report that some become worse. However, the majority of studies in this review indicated that, when the sexually abused children in treatment were compared with non-abused children in treatment, the sexually abused were less symptomatic than their nonabused clinical counterparts. In addition, the majority of those showing psychological harm improved markedly within 12 to 18 months *with or without* treatment.

Outrageous Testimony

Referring to the Salem witch trials, U.S. Supreme Court Justice Louis Brandeis once said that the judges in 1692 Massachusetts prosecuted witches, "but burnt women." At these present-day child abuse trials, very young children testified they had been cooked in a microwave oven, seen babies murdered by their tormenters, and been taken for orgies on spaceships around the moon. And prosecutors, juries, and judges—seeing nothing too aberrational in such testimony—locked up the defendants.

Nat Hentoff, *Editor & Publisher*, January 1, 2001.

In an earlier review of 28 studies, A. Browne and D. Finkelhor (1986) concluded that, when studied as adults, less than 20% of those who had been sexually abused as children had serious psychopathology as adults. Browne and Finkelhor observed that these findings should provide comfort to victims since severe long-term effects were not inevitable. They note with concern the efforts of child advocates to exaggerate the harmful effects for political purposes because of its potential to harm the victims and their families.

That the claims of harm are exaggerated and, indeed, may well be inaccurate is substantiated in a landmark study by B. Rind and P. Tromovitch (1997). These researchers noted that most of the prior reviews had drawn upon clinical and legal samples, which are not representative of the general population. They conducted a meta-analysis of seven studies that used national probability samples, which are more appropriate for making population-relevant inferences. The studies included four from the United States, and one each from Great Britain, Canada, and Spain. Their findings indicated that harm from child sexual abuse is not pervasive among those who experienced early sexual experiences. Further, the harm, when it occurs, is not serious.

These findings confirm the earlier findings of A.C. Kinsey and his associates (1953) who found that, among those participants (24%) who had had sexual contact with adults in their childhood, 80% recalled being emotionally upset by these contacts. However, in all but a few cases, the negative effect was "nearer the level that children will show when they see insects, spiders, or other objects against which they have been adversely conditioned."

Moreover, Rind and Tromovitch's meta-analysis supports the view that the behaviors and attitudes exhibited by the sexually abused are unlikely to be the effects of the sexual abuse. They may be the result, instead, of preexisting problems, or even of professional and community intervention, as earlier reported by Constantine (1981).

Further, there is no sound research supporting the stereotypical linkage of child sexual abuse and later adult psychopathology. Existing research in this regard is so seriously methodologically flawed that it is virtually valueless, according to H.G. Pope and J.I. Hudson (1995). A similar conclusion was arrived at by staff of the False Memory Foundation who, with the help of members of the Foundation's Scientific Advisory Committee, analyzed the research in this area. They identified the assumption that childhood sexual abuse results in the development of psychiatric disorders in adulthood as a leading candidate to join the ranks of other mental health myths. They noted that:

> to question the pathogenic effects of childhood sexual abuse is often considered heretical—just as it would have been scandalous, a generation ago, to question whether bad mothering could turn children into schizophrenics.

It is, in fact, far from proven that childhood sexual abuse has any significant influence upon the adult personality. As noted by M.E.P. Seligman (1994), adults are not prisoners of their past, even a past marked by childhood trauma.

That child sexual abuse may not be harmful is not to condone it or to suggest that it should not be considered either immoral or illegal or both. J.R. Conte (1985) has pointed out that decisions concerning the appropriateness of adult/ nonadult sexual interactions involve ethical, legal, and religious principles. By way of example, robbery is unlawful not because it results in psychological harm but because society has decided that people have a right to their own property. Put another way, the question of the effects of child sexual abuse should not be confused with the moral and/or legal issue of dealing with this behavior.

The Therapy Marketeer

The final indicator suggesting a professional may be a child saver is when the professional acts as a *therapy marketeer*, exaggerating the need for therapy for the victims of sexual abuse. From 44% to 73% of victims are likely to receive some form of psychotherapy. This, of course, is in line with a belief in the trauma ideology.

Many children, however, are referred to therapy who do not need to be. The fact that significant numbers of the sexually abused are not psychologically harmed and those who are improve within a year or two without any treatment attests to the minimal need, if any, for therapy. Thus, the concern expressed by the San Diego Grand Jury (1992, February) that referrals to therapists were simply "feeding another subindustry of the System" is well founded. The approach of the psychotherapeutic community to child sexual abuse reflects a mental health industry searching for a new disease which offers it new opportunities for economic growth.

Further, there is no sound research evidence indicating that therapy for the sexually abused is effective. E. Holenberg and C. Ragan (1991) reported in their synthesis of selected research projects funded by the National Center on Child Abuse and Neglect that most of the information on treatment efficacy was based on anecdotal case studies or descriptions of treatment programs.

Most treatment programs are either atheoretical or based

on untested theoretical assumptions. And this is to the ever-lasting harm of some. For example, in the Alicia Wade case, it was as a result of her therapist's brainwashing in over a year of so-called therapy involving twice weekly visits that Alicia finally "disclosed" that her father had raped her. In fact, as Alicia had previously maintained, she had been raped by a stranger—and it turned out he was a serial rapist!

Lest this be seen as idiosyncratic, a recently completed evaluation of repressed memory claims with the State of Washington's Crime Victims Compensation Program clearly indicates the potential for the harm that can be inflicted by therapy. Some therapists believe that childhood sexual abuse is a central experience in the lives of their clients. They contend that the trauma of child sexual abuse motivates the patients to repress this experience. Given the centrality of this experience, these therapists assume it is necessary for their patients to recover previously repressed memories of their sexual abuse if they are to heal.

But quite the opposite can occur, as indicated by L.E. Parr's (1996) study. She reported that patients involved in repressed memory therapy displayed:

> an unusually high rate of mental and emotional problems which manifest during therapy and are proliferated as therapy continues. Repressed memory patients tend to be in therapy significantly longer than other mental health clients but with little improvement in their conditions even after years of therapy. Indeed, it appears that the longer the patient is [in] treatment, the more disabled s(he) will become. Of significant concern is that over the course of time, repressed memory patients often become isolated from their families and communities, suffer employment and financial losses and demonstrate devastating mental problems which diminishes their capacity to form or maintain meaningful relationships or enjoy life.

Moreover, anecdotal case studies show that therapists have implanted memories of childhood sexual abuse that never occurred.

Additionally, there is growing evidence that the recent epidemic of Multiple Personality Disorder (MPD) is an artifact of therapy. It is a therapist-induced disorder rather than an effect of child sexual abuse. Parr (1996) reported that the primary diagnosis in most repressed memory claims to the Crime Victims Compensation Program was MPD and that it was not unusual for the claimant to have dozens or even hundreds of personalities—one claim involved over 700 alter states and another over 3000. Parr's findings buttress the conclusion of R. Ofshe and E. Watters:

> Examining the fad diagnosis of MPD, the cruelty of recovered memory therapy becomes particularly clear. Thousands of clients have learned to display the often-debilitating symptoms of a disorder that they never had. They become less capable of living normal lives, more dependent on therapy, and inevitably more troubled.

Lastly, there is no evidence that reliving the abuse experience has any positive effects. Seligman (1994) notes that, although catharsis has a long history as a therapeutic technique, there is no evidence that it works. He adds that efforts by parents and well-meaning therapists and courts of law often magnify the trauma in the child's mind by repeatedly tearing off the protective scar tissue of the wound. Thus, these well-intentioned people are actually interfering with the natural healing process.

"Savers" Who Harm

In brief, child savers are those professionals who purport to protect victims of child sexual abuse but who instead harm them and devastate the lives of families. They have certain beliefs which are red flags for identifying them: 1) a *proselytizer* who spreads the false gospel of satanic ritual abuse; 2) a *validator* who confirms uncorroborated allegations of sexual abuse no matter how bizarre; 3) an *exaggerator* or user of advocacy numbers; 4) a *trauma ideologist;* and 5) a *therapy marketeer.* . . .

Child sexual abuse is both immoral and illegal and should be condemned. But there is another form of abuse—this is the abuse perpetrated by the child savers. This abuse devastates the lives of individuals and families. It too must be condemned.

"More than 70 priests in the archdiocese of Boston—out of a total of less than 700—have been accused of the sexual abuse of children."

Child Sexual Abuse by Priests Is Widespread

Andrew Sullivan

Andrew Sullivan claims in the following viewpoint that for years the Catholic Church has covered up systematic child sexual abuse by priests. He argues that the church has hushed up sex scandals, paid secret damages to victims, and moved pedophile priests to other parishes, where they usually abuse again. Sullivan charges the church with hypocrisy for preaching a strict doctrine governing sexuality while allowing sexual abuse within the church to flourish. Andrew Sullivan is a senior editor of the weekly magazine *New Republic* and author of the book *Virtually Normal: An Argument About Homosexuality*.

As you read, consider the following questions:

1. According to Sullivan, what types of sexual activity does the Catholic Church condemn?
2. What ratio of priests does Sullivan calculate have been accused of sexually abusing children?
3. As stated by the author, in what ways is the Catholic Church sexually dysfunctional?

The Roman Catholic Church holds as an important doctrine that sexuality, though a gift from God, is fraught with moral danger. There is also only one legitimate form of sexual expression—a married heterosexual relationship, always open to the possibility of procreation. So the nature of sex is inescapably bound up with the creation of new life, and any attempt to get around that nature, any variation upon it, is a violation of what God intends. The church therefore condemns masturbation for the same reason that it condemns homosexual sex and contraception. And Catholic doctrine also bars divorce, because it violates the integrity of marriage, which, by definition, can happen only once in a lifetime.

This position has integrity, even though it can seem at times cruel and alien to much of human experience. Most of us know that the force of sexuality, perhaps the most powerful in human life, regularly breaks through such narrow boundaries. But the church insists that its prohibitions are not intended to isolate or wound the divorced, or homosexuals or teenagers in love. Its doctrinal rigidity is maintained out of compassion and besides, the church has no other choice than to uphold the truth, however painful for those caught in humanity's crooked timber.

I suppose it is partly this context that makes the pedophile-priest scandal in Boston [that began in February 2002] so offensive to so many. . . . It has been revealed that more than 70 priests in the archdiocese of Boston—out of a total of less than 700—have been accused of the sexual abuse of children. That's 1 in 10. Worse, when evidence of these crimes has come to light, the church hierarchy has done everything in its power to hush it up, pay secret damages to the victims and, in many cases, do nothing but reassign pedophile priests to other parishes, where they can commit abuse again. In one of the worst cases, that of the Reverend John Geoghan, the church hierarchy had responded to clear evidence of his depravity by moving the now defrocked priest around for almost two decades—as he continued his pattern of molestation of minors. [In February 2002] he was sentenced to nine to 10 years for indecent assault and battery.

How can a church that preaches the impermissibility of so

many forms of consensual, adult sex simultaneously tolerate, ignore or cover up the sexual abuse of children by its own priests? Pedophilia is not a failing; it is not some imperfect but victimless expression of sexuality among consenting adults. It is a crime. To my mind, the violation of a child's innocence, the betrayal of a priestly trust, the rape of a minor's very body provide about as good a definition of evil as one can find. Yet a church that regularly condemns and judges so many of its congregants for comparatively minor sexual variations on the married heterosexual norm permits and covers up far worse offenses among its own.

Branch. © 1993 *San Antonio Express News*. Reprinted by permission of John Branch.

And they still don't get it. Yes, Cardinal Bernard Law has formally apologized. But his reckoning was carefully parsed. "In retrospect," Law said in his formal statement, the "response of the archdiocese to the grave evil . . . was flawed and inadequate." In retrospect? By what conceivable moral argument could ignoring child abuse be deemed at any time acceptable? "In retrospect," he also said, he had put children in danger, "albeit unintentionally." How can a church demand moral responsibility of its members if its leaders cannot do so when unmitigated evil is standing right in front of them?

This is not a liberal or conservative issue. Sure, liberal Catholics see the scandal as another indicator of the sexual dysfunction at the heart of the church. And they have a point. Celibacy is an onerous burden that can easily distort a person's psyche. Moreover, many sexually conflicted men gravitate to the priesthood precisely because it promises to put a straitjacket on their compulsions and confusions. Alas, that straitjacket can often come undone. The absence of women in the higher reaches of the church further distorts the atmosphere; and the presence of large numbers of gay priests—forced to preach against their very identity and fight against their own need for love—only intensifies the psychological pressure of the priesthood. But conservatives are just as outraged. The abuse of children rightly provokes horror among traditional Catholics, and they have been admirably reluctant to close ranks behind the corrupted hierarchy. Besides, the most devout and trusting have often been the most victimized. "After he molested me, he would bless me," a former altar boy, abused in the Los Angeles diocese, recently told the *Los Angeles Times*. "It's very confusing. I was in the center of my mother's life—the church—and she thought I was doing constructive things by being with the priest. After we did these things, he'd put his hand on my head and make the sign of the cross."

This isn't a failing of the church; it's an attack upon its integrity—by its own clergy. Until this evil is rooted out—and until the culpable bishops and cardinals who tolerated it resign—it will surely be hard for American Catholics to trust or love their church again.

*"The numbers of priests involved in such
criminal activity are few."*

Child Sexual Abuse by Priests
Is Not Widespread

Wilton D. Gregory

Wilton D. Gregory is a bishop from Belleville, Illinois, and
president of the U.S. Conference of Catholic Bishops. In the
following viewpoint, which was originally released on
February 19, 2002, as a statement on the sexual abuse of minors by priests, Gregory contends that few priests have been
involved in child sexual abuse. According to Gregory, the
vast majority of priests work hard for society and for the
church. He claims that the Catholic Church is recognized by
many as the leading institution working to understand and
address the sexual abuse of minors.

As you read, consider the following questions:
1. According to Gregory, what steps has the Catholic
   Church taken to deal with priests who have been
   accused of abuse?
2. What policies and programs have Catholic bishops
   implemented to help address sexual abuse in the church,
   as stated by the author?
3. Approximately how many priests are there in the United
   States, according to the author?

In [February 2002] our attention has again been turned to the issue of sexual abuse of minors by priests. Though the renewed focus on this issue is due largely to cases of priest abusers that were not dealt with appropriately in the past, it gives me the occasion as a pastor and a teacher of faith and morals to express, on behalf of all of the bishops, our profound sorrow that some of our priests were responsible for this abuse under our watch. We understand that your children are your most precious gift. They are our children as well, and we continue to apologize to the victims and to their parents and their loved ones for this failure in our pastoral responsibilities.

The Church Is Successfully Addressing Sexual Abuse

The attention to this issue also gives me the opportunity to renew the promise of our bishops that we will continue to take all the steps necessary to protect our youth from this kind of abuse in society and in the church. While we still have much for which we need to be forgiven—and much to learn—I am very heartened by the professionals who work with both victims and abusers who encourage us in this work because, they tell us, there is not another institution in the United States that is doing more to understand and address the horror of sexual abuse of minors.

As a church, we have met with those who are victims of sexual abuse by priests. We have heard their sorrow, confusion, anger and fear. We have tried to reach out pastorally and sensitively not only to victims of this outrageous behavior, but to their families and the communities devastated by this crime. We have confronted priests accused of abuse and removed them from public ministry.

Over the past two decades, the bishops of the United States have worked diligently to learn all we can about sexual abuse. Our conference has encouraged the development of policies in every diocese to address this issue. Bishops have developed procedures whereby priests moving from one diocese to another must have certification of their good standing. Bishops have also revised seminary screening and have mandated in-service programs for priests, teachers, parish ministers and volunteers to emphasize their responsibility to protect the innocent and vulnerable from such abuse. Dioceses have implemented programs to ensure safe environments in parishes and schools. While we have made some tragic mistakes, we have attempted to be as honest and open about these cases as we can, especially in following the law on these matters and cooperating with civil authorities. We remain committed to seeing these initiatives implemented fully, because the church must be a place of refuge and security, not a place of denial and distress. Sadly, we are faced with the fact that evil does harm the innocent, something which human life has faced since the beginning of time. This is a reality against which we must be ceaselessly on guard.

A Few Bad Apples

I want to say a word about the more than 40,000 wonderful priests in our country who get up every morning to give their lives in full service to the church as witnesses to Jesus Christ in our midst. I am very saddened that the crimes of a few have cast a shadow over the grace-filled and necessary work that they do day in and day out for society and for the church. The priesthood is a unique treasure of our church, and I give you my assurance that we are doing everything to ensure that we have worthy and healthy candidates for the priesthood and to strengthen the many priests who faithfully fulfill their ministry on behalf of all of us.

While we deplore the sexual abuse of young people, especially that committed by a cleric, we are confident that the numbers of priests involved in such criminal activity are few. The damage, however, has been immeasurable. The toll this phenomenon has taken on our people and our ministry is tremendous. This is a time for Catholic people, bishops, clergy, religious and laity, to resolve anew to work together to assure the safety of our children. These events serve to remind us all that the cost of preventing these terrible misdeeds in the future is a careful watch that cannot and will not be relaxed. We bishops intend to maintain that watch together with and on behalf of our people.

As we pursue this common work for the safety of our children and for the good of society and the church we love, let us continue to remember one another before the Lord in prayer and in charity.

Periodical Bibliography

The following articles have been selected to supplement the diverse views presented in this chapter.

William J. Bennett	"A Travesty of Protecting Priests, Not the Victims," *San Diego Union-Tribune*, April 7, 2002.
Edward Egan	"Sexual Abuse of Children: Immoral, Illegal, and an Abomination," *Origins*, April 4, 2002.
Fear Us	"Rape," 2001. www.fearus.org.
Kevin M. Gorey and Donald R. Leslie	"Working Toward a Valid Prevalence Estimate of Child Sexual Abuse: A Reply to Bolen and Scannapieco," *Social Service Review*, March 2001.
Joseph J. Guido	"The Importance of Perspective: Understanding the Sexual Abuse of Children by Priests," *America*, April 1, 2002.
Harvard Mental Health Letter	"In Brief—Is Child Sexual Abuse Declining?" January 2002.
Nat Hentoff	"Getting It Right," *Editor & Publisher*, January 1, 2001.
Lottie L. Joiner	"Healing the Scars," *Emerge*, May 1997.
National Catholic Reporter	"Scandal's Cure Lies in Tackling Deeper Issues," March 22, 2002.
Richard John Neuhaus	"Consequences of a False Sense of Compassion," *San Diego Union-Tribune*, April 7, 2002.
Joseph Perkins	"Revamped Rules of Romance," *Washington Times*, June 10, 1997.
Anna Quindlen	"Patent Leather, Impure Thoughts: The Obsession with Sins of the Flesh Helped Lead the Catholic Church into This Disaster," *Newsweek*, April 1, 2002.
Tina Rosenberg	"New Punishments for an Ancient War Crime," *New York Times*, April 5, 1998.
Brenda L. Shapiro and J. Conrad Schwarz	"Date Rape: Its Relationship to Trauma Symptoms and Sexual Self-Esteem," *Journal of Interpersonal Violence*, 1997.
Carol Tavris	"Uproar Over Sexual Abuse Study Muddies the Waters," *Los Angeles Times*, July 19, 1999.

CHAPTER 3

How Should Society Address Sexual Victimization?

Chapter Preface

Maggie, a character in Tennessee Williams's *Cat on a Hot Tin Roof*, declares, "When something is festering in your memory . . . laws of silence don't work. . . . Silence about a thing just magnifies it. It grows and festers in silence, becomes malignant." Actress Elizabeth Ashley, who played Maggie in a 1974 production, agrees. She was raped in 1977 but did not reveal the crime or deal with the resulting emotional devastation until 1993, when she testified at the sentencing of the man convicted of raping her longtime friend. Ashley noted, "By breaking my silence, I can finally begin to make peace with the rage in my soul."

According to many victims of rape and other forms of sexual assault, publicly sharing stories of abuse can help a woman recover from the ordeal. As Ashley explains, "Talking about what happened to me has been cathartic." After she was raped repeatedly by three men who accosted her at a remote gas station near Bakersfield, California, she decided to try to forget the incident, but her life seemed to fall apart anyway. Belatedly, Ashley realized that because she had never told anyone about the rape, she had denied herself the opportunity to work through its emotional consequences. When the actress finally announced during her friend's trial that she had been gang raped, she was able to start the mending process.

Like Ashley, Maureen O'Boyle, who was host of the syndicated TV series *A Current Affair*, was also raped, but, unlike the actress, she reacted by immediately telling the police, her family, and coworkers about the incident. According to O'Boyle, a man broke into her apartment one night in 1986 and raped her for over three hours. O'Boyle immediately called the police and then went to stay with her parents to recuperate. Her coworkers also knew of the rape and were supportive, and her boss generously allowed her time off to recover. O'Boyle advises, "If it [rape] happens to you, tell someone right away. There is nothing to be ashamed of: It's not your fault." Failure to work through the feelings of fear and betrayal can also prevent a rape victim from entering into intimate relationships. O'Boyle says, "Telling my story is part of getting close to somebody. I don't go out with men who don't understand what happened to me."

Ashley and O'Boyle are high-profile women whose stories eventually became public knowledge. Of course, ordinary women get raped, too, and although their stories do not always get published in leading magazines, they do voice their tales of abuse in order to facilitate the healing process. In the following chapter, authors discuss several ways sexual victimization can be addressed, including the public proclamation of abuse. Echoing the advice of Tennessee Williams's Maggie, teacher and activist Suzanne Stutman proclaims, "We must raise our voices into the darkness so that . . . no victims surrender in silence and shame."

> "Instead of dismissing victim stories as individual whining . . . , I am interested in how stories of personal suffering can be used as a means of building public empathy [for women]."

Women Should Tell Their Stories of Sexual Victimization

Martha T. McCluskey

Martha T. McCluskey contends in the following viewpoint that sharing stories of sexual victimization can empower women and generate public empathy toward victims. According to McCluskey, despite accusations that feminists exaggerate the extent of female victimization, systematic public denial about the seriousness of violence against women is rampant. Ironically, she maintains, men are now claiming to be the victims of feminist excesses while at the same time enjoying the power and privilege to which they have traditionally been entitled. McCluskey edited, with Martha A. Fineman, the book *Feminism, Media, and the Law*.

As you read, consider the following questions:
1. Why did Colby College ban fraternities in 1984, as stated by McCluskey?
2. According to the author's victim story, what happened to her at Colby College in 1977?
3. In McCluskey's opinion, what are the two prevailing stereotypes of women?

Martha T. McCluskey, "Transforming Victimization," *Tikkun*, vol. 9, March/April 1994, pp. 54–57. Copyright © 1994 by Martha T. McCluskey. Reproduced by permission.

Violence against women by middle- or upperclass white men traditionally has been invisible in the public eye. Systematic public denial is the foundation of many of the horrors of modern times. Yet how can we reveal and heal previously hidden injustices, such as domestic violence, acquaintance rape, and sexual harassment, without contributing to the dominant story, which casts women as inevitably damaged and vulnerable to male control? And how can we publicly validate previously silenced personal pain without institutionalizing new forms of unproductive silence?

Instead of dismissing victim stories as individual whining that breeds division and cynicism at worst or paternalistic protection at best, I am interested in how stories of personal suffering can be used as a means of building public empathy.

Feminist Victimization

Recently, media attention has focused on the "feminist victimization" problem on college campuses in the context of date-rape education programs and rules governing hate speech and sexual conduct. In this discussion, heterosexual white men at elite colleges are often presented as newly silenced victims of feminist excess and repression. And some people worry that such a focus on women college students as victims of sexual violence will perpetuate antifeminist stereotypes of white, economically privileged women as sexually passive and helpless.

My view is that narratives of women's sexual victimization can in some circumstances be used to establish women as empowered and responsible agents. After all, those who identify with privileged male authority have always had it both ways: Our legal system is testament to their success at positioning themselves as both victims and agents. Supreme Court justice Clarence Thomas, for example, achieved his position of supreme public authority through a story of his personal suffering as "high-tech lynching" victim [when Anita Hill accused him of sexual harassment in 1991]. It is not the subject matter of one's story—victimization—but rather one's position as authoritative subject that determines whether or not narratives of harm bolster or undermine one's power and autonomy. As an example, I'm going to talk about victim stories

in one dispute about "political correctness" on college campuses—a lawsuit challenging Colby College's decision to
prohibit students from belonging to fraternities.

Colby (a small, selective liberal arts school in Maine)
banned fraternities and sororities in 1984 as a response to
the fraternities' history of sexism, harassment, vandalism,
and other problems. In 1990, after six years of continuing
problems with fraternities that continued to flourish under-
ground despite the ban, the college punished a group of students for participating in the initiation rituals of a fraternity
called Lambda Chi Alpha. The college barred the Lambda
Chi seniors from marching in graduation ceremonies and
suspended the other members for one semester.

The Maine Civil Liberties Union then initiated a lawsuit
on behalf of the punished fraternity members under a new
state human rights law. The Civil Liberties Union claimed
that the college violated the fraternity members' First
Amendment freedom of association rights. In media stories
about the lawsuit, the Civil Liberties Union and national
fraternity leaders portrayed the fraternity ban as part of a
dangerous new wave of intolerance sweeping the country, as
colleges force "politically correct" views on students as a result of feminist complaints.

One Victim's Story

In response, I wrote several essays for local media raising the
question of whether some Colby College fraternities might
possibly be hate groups in which membership might in some
circumstances have the effect of limiting others' equally important freedoms. My essays about the fraternity case were
in part a story of my own victimization as a student at Colby.
I'm going to repeat a part of my victim story here as an example of the feminist victimization problem. By telling this
story, I'm acting out the victim/agency contradiction which
I want to transform: I'm positioning myself as silenced victim of misogynist violence and at the same time as speaking
author attempting to rewrite the framework within which
my victimization is told.

It is 1977 at Colby College. I'm a student living on Third
Floor Dana. Most of the guys on our hall are pledging

Lambda Chi and KDR, rumored to be the worst fraternities on campus—and the most prestigious.

It's the beginning of a vacation and my dorm is quiet and nearly empty. I am standing in the hallway looking out the window for my ride home. I turn around and my suitcase is gone; Joe and Bill from down the hall are laughing as they carry it away. I follow them. I hear a door lock behind me. They let go of my suitcase and grab me.

I am lying on the bare linoleum floor of Joe's bedroom. In the room are a group of Lambda Chi and KDR pledges who live on my hall; several of them are football players. Some are sitting on the bed, laughing. Two others are pinning my arms and my legs to the floor. Joe is touching me while the others cheer.

I am a friendly fellow-classmate as I reasonably explain that I'm in a rush to catch a ride; that I'm not in the mood to joke around; that I'd really like them to please cut it out. It takes a few long upside-down seconds before things look different. As I start to scream and fight, they let me go.

Later I don't talk about this, not even to myself. I sit near Joe and Bill in sociology and English classes. I don't talk in class.

Victim Narratives

I used this and other stories of misogynist victimization by Colby fraternity members to try to raise the question of harm to women and other students caused by fraternity membership, a question that had been until then completely left out of the media discussion of the fraternity lawsuit. But the critics of "victim feminism" are right that, interpreted as a confession of my victimization in itself, my story is risky.

The traditional stereotype of certain women as passive sexual victims is inseparable from the traditional stereotype about "other" women as sinister sexual agents. To the extent my victim story is compelling, it reveals my exercise of authority as illegitimately powerful emotional manipulation, while at the same time it shows that I am an emotional, vulnerable female who needs protection from responsible, rigorous debate. Placed within the dominant civil libertarian framework, when I speak about fraternity violence against women, I'm talking about emotional personal experience. In contrast, those who speak about college restrictions on men's right to associate as fraternity brothers are invoking rational universal principles.

Ways Women Can Protect Themselves from Sexual Victimization

- 68% of women reported that they routinely locked their doors when alone.
- 58% planned their route for reasons of safety.
- 58% checked the back seat of their parked car before getting in.
- 24% stayed at home at night.
- 17% carried some kind of weapon.

Timmons and Area Women in Crisis, 1993, http://crisis.vianet.on.ca.

Victim narratives starring privileged heterosexual men are central to establishing the legitimacy of their demands for protection. Reporting on Colby's decision to enforce its ban on fraternities by suspending (not expelling) the members for one semester, a national fraternity leader complained that Colby's president "and his hand-picked thought police regiment have advanced repression to new heights . . . making it a crime punishable by expulsion to be a heterosexual male who chooses to formalize his friendship with other like-minded friends away from campus." Reaching even further, one fraternity member's letter printed in the campus newspaper declared that the college's ban on fraternities was a "form of genocide" comparable to the Holocaust and the Cambodian killing fields.

There's been a flurry of books and media discussions recently which have widely questioned whether feminists' efforts to stop public denial of sexual violence has led to careless use of the terms "rape" and "sexual harassment." Why isn't there a similarly hot market for books and talk shows urging a heterosexual white male audience to be scrupulously self-critical when they talk about their concerns about feminist tactics?

Privilege and Oppression

Indeed, victim narratives by those with social privilege often work to deny responsibility for the social agency that results from that privilege, cleverly making the most privileged people deserving of the greatest legal protection for their suffering. A law journal article cited by fraternity lawyers in the Colby case pointed to evidence of widespread fraternity violence against women as proof that fraternity men suffer from lower self-confidence than college women—suggesting that as a result fraternity men are more disadvantaged and more in need of special legal rights than the women they assault.

Critics of "victim feminism" argue that many women shrink from identifying with feminism because of the indignity of the victim role that feminists present. *Newsweek's* cover story on "Sexual Correctness" on campus acknowledges statistics showing college women are at high risk of sexual assault but then comments: "You want to talk victimization? Talk to the mothers all over America whose children have been slaughtered in urban cross-fire."

Such criticisms tend not to challenge the identification of victims of oppression as pathetic and impotent, but instead aim to simply displace the traditional negative victim image from elite college women onto "others" supposedly distant in terms of race, class, religion, ethnicity, or mental ability. Instead of drawing lines between authentic helpless "victims" and tough empowered "agents," we need to question this dichotomy and recognize that we each share a complicated and contextual mixture of identities of privilege and oppression.

Victim stories alone are not transformative, just as they are not in themselves victimizing. Speaking out about personal pain should be viewed not as an unquestionable revelation of authentic inner experience, but as one honorable way of asserting public power, carrying with it the responsibilities and dangers of such power. By telling my victim story publicly, my goal is not to claim an absolute status as oppressed, nor to inspire apologetic expressions of sympathy or affirmation, but to provoke a rigorous and respectful debate about the line between speech and conduct and to examine the ways perceptions of harm are socially constructed. In order to shape more compassionate and responsible communities with less pain and more pleasure, victim narratives should be a starting point for questioning our assumptions about when we need to accept our fears and our pain as part of giving up privilege and learning to recognize others' sometimes conflicting needs, and when instead we can responsibly demand a community response to our pain as a matter of public principle.

"Proclaiming victimhood doesn't help project strength."

Women Should Avoid Claiming Status as Victims

Katie Roiphe

In the following viewpoint, Katie Roiphe argues that anti-rape demonstrations—such as the annual "Take Back the Night" marches held on many college campuses—encourage women to view themselves as actual or potential victims of sexual violence. Roiphe maintains that by speaking publicly about their victimization and their feelings of helplessness, activists at these demonstrations reinforce the stereotype that women are weak and vulnerable. Promoting this negative stereotype is not a constructive way to deal with the problem of sexual violence, she concludes. Roiphe is the author of *The Morning After: Sex, Fear, and Feminism on Campus*, from which this viewpoint is excerpted.

As you read, consider the following questions:
1. According to Roiphe, how are the speakers' stories at the "Take Back the Night" marches similar?
2. How does John Irving's *The World According to Garp* illustrate some feminists' obsession with "being silenced," in Roiphe's opinion?
3. According to the author, why did Mindy, the "Take Back the Night" march participant, falsely accuse a male student of rape?

Katie Roiphe, *The Morning After: Sex, Fear, and Feminism on Campus*. New York: Little, Brown and Company, 1993. Copyright © 1993 by Katherine Anne Roiphe. Reproduced by permission of the publisher.

It's April—leaves sprouting, flowers, mad crushes, flirta-tions, Chaucer's pilgrims, bare legs, long days, and marches against rape. Renewal means more than those prac-tically obscene magnolia trees again, branches laden with Georgia O'Keeffe blossoms. Renewal means more than pass-ing exams and drinking wine outside. It means more than en-joying the lengthening day: it means taking back the night.

A March Against Sexual Violence

It's a Saturday night. It's the end of the month and it still hasn't gotten warm. Instead of listening to bands, or watch-ing movies, or drinking beer, more than four hundred Princeton students are "taking back the night." That is, they are marching, as one of the organizers says into the micro-phone, "to end sexual violence against women." In past years the numbers have climbed to a thousand participants. Car-rying candles, the students march through campus, past the library, and down Prospect Street, past the eating clubs, the social hub of Princeton's undergraduates.

The marchers chant "Princeton unite, take back the night, Princeton unite, take back the night," and a drumbeat adds drama, noise, and substance to their voices. As they pass the eating clubs the chants get louder, more forceful. "No matter what we wear, no matter where we go, yes means yes and no means no!" It's already dark. They scheduled the march earlier this year, because last year's march went until three in the morning. "Hey ho! Hey ho! Sexism has got to go." As they march, girls put their arms around each other. Some of the march organizers wear armbands. This is to identify them in case anyone falls apart and needs to talk.

The ritual is this: at various points in the march everyone stops and gathers around the microphone. Then the "sur-vivors" and occasionally the friends of "survivors" get up to "speak out." One by one they take their place at the micro-phone, and one by one they tell their story. The stories are intimate accounts of sexual violence, ranging from being afraid on the subway to having been the victim of gang rape and incest.

The marchers stand in Prospect Garden, a flower garden behind the faculty club. A short, plump girl who looks like she is barely out of high school cups her hands around the microphone. Her face is pink from the cold. She begins to describe a party at one of the eating clubs. Her words are slow, loud, deliberate. That night, she had more beers than she could remember, and she was too drunk to know what was going on. A boy she knew was flirting with her, he asked her to go back to his room—it all happened so fast. Her friends told her not to. They told her she was too drunk to make decisions. She went anyway, and he raped her. Later, she says, his roommates thought he was cool for "hooking up." She left her favorite blue jean jacket in his room. She finally went and got it back, but she never wore it again. She pauses. Later the boy apologized to her, so, she says angrily, he must have known it was rape. She stops talking and looks into the crowd. Everyone applauds to show their support.

As the applause dies down, another girl stands up, her face shiny with tears, and brushes the blond hair out of her eyes. I wasn't going to speak out, she explains, because I wasn't a survivor of rape, but I too was silenced. A friend, she continues, someone I used to have a crush on, betrayed my trust. We were lying next to each other and he touched my body. She pauses, swallowing the tears rising in her throat, then goes on: I didn't say anything, I was too embarrassed to say or do anything. I just pretended I was asleep. Distraught, confused, she talks in circles for a while, not sure where her story is leading her, and finally walks away from the microphone.

The next girl to speak out wears a leather jacket and black jeans. People think of me as a bitch, she says, her voice loud, confident, angry, they think of me as a slut. They think I treat men badly. But she explains that underneath her bitchiness is a gang rape that happened when she was sixteen. So if you see someone who acts like me, you shouldn't judge them or hate them, she says. Considering what happened to me I am in good shape, she says, I'm doing really well. It's just fucking great that I can even have orgasms. As she leaves the microphone, her friends put their arms around her. . . .

A Similarity Among Victims' Stories
The strange thing is that as these different girls—tall and short, fat and thin, nervous and confident—get up to give in-

tensely personal accounts, all of their stories begin to sound the same. Listening to a string of them, I hear patterns begin to emerge. The same phrases float through different voices. Almost all of them begin "I wasn't planning to speak out tonight but . . . ," even the ones who had spoken in previous years. They talk about feeling helpless, and feeling guilty. Some talk about hating their bodies. The echoes continue: "I didn't admit it or talk about it." "I was silenced." "I was powerless over my own body."

The catchwords travel across campuses, and across the boundaries between the spoken and written word. In a piece in the most radical of Harvard's feminist magazines, the *Rag*, one student asks, "Why should I have to pay with silence for a crime committed against my body? . . . I want you to know how it feels to be denied your own voice." Voicelessness is a common motif in Take Back the Night speak-outs. In 1988 the *Daily Princetonian* quoted one speaker as saying, "Victims shouldn't be silenced." At Berkeley, students organized a group designed to combat sexual assault called Coalition to Break the Silence. In the *Nassau Weekly*, Jennifer Goode, a Princeton sophomore, writes that Take Back the Night "counteracts the enforced silence of everyday existence. . . . This Saturday night the silence will be broken."

The Popularity of "Being Silenced"

These Princeton women, future lawyers, newspaper reporters, investment bankers, are hardly the voiceless, by most people's definition. But silence is poetic. Being silenced is even more poetic. These days people vie for the position of being silenced, but being silenced is necessarily a construction of the articulate. Once you're talking about being voiceless, you're already talking. The first Take Back the Night march at Princeton was more than ten years ago, and every year they're breaking the silence all over again. The fashionable cloak of silence is more about style than content.

Built into the rhetoric about silence is the image of a malign force clamping its hands over the mouths of victims. This shadowy force takes on many names—patriarchy, men, society—but with such abstract quantities in the formula, it's hard to fathom the meaning behind the metaphor. It doesn't matter, though. Almost all of the victims continue to talk about their silence.

It is the presumption of silence that gives these women the right to speak, that elevates their words above the competitive noise of the university. Silence is the passkey to the empowering universe of the disempowered. Having been silenced on today's campus is the ultimate source of authority.

Excluding Half the Community

Many critics have chastised the Take Back the Night (TBTN) March because of sexual segregation. They argue that while the Ann Arbor Coalition Against Rape (AACAR) acknowledges rape as both a "community" and a "human" issue in their public rhetoric, the march repudiates these claims by excluding half of the community and half of humanity. They make the point that, if AACAR wants rape to be viewed as an issue which requires everyone's attention and action, then they should want as many people, both men and women, as possible to participate in the TBTN March.

C.J. Carnacchio, *Michigan Review*, April 21, 1999.

One of the most scathing condemnations of the long-standing feminist obsession with silence comes from John Irving. In *The World According to Garp*, Irving tells the story of Ellen James, a modern-day Philomela: she was raped at the age of eleven, and her tongue was cut out by the rapist. Much to Garp's dismay, a group of feminists springs up around her, cutting out their own tongue in a gesture of political solidarity. They communicate through notes: "I am an Ellen Jamesian." They hold meetings and take stands. They dedicate themselves to the cause. When Ellen James herself reappears in the novel as an adult, she confesses that she hates the Ellen Jamesians. Beneath his comic, excessive, grotesque image of this feminist clan, Irving makes a realistic point about the feminist preoccupation with silence. He takes the political reality of feminists' insistence on identification with victims one step further: his feminists are so eager to declare themselves silenced that they are actually willing to cut out their own tongue.

As I listen to the refrains, "I have been silent," "I was silenced," "I am finally breaking the silence," the speakers begin to blur together in my mind. It makes sense that rape victims experience some similar reactions, but what is strange is that they choose the same words. Somehow the individual power of each story is sapped by the collective mode of expression. The individual details fade, the stories blend together, sounding programmed and automatic. As I listen to them I am reminded of the scene in Madeleine L'Engle's children's book *A Wrinkle in Time* in which a row of identical children play outside of a row of identical houses, bouncing a row of identical balls.

The *Rag*'s account of a rape ends "Thanks [to] the rest of you for listening," and an account published in the *Daily Princetonian* ends "Thank you for listening." As the vocabulary shared across campuses reveals, there is an archetype, a model, for the victim's tale. Take Back the Night speak-outs follow conventions as strict as any sonnet sequence or villanelle. As intimate details are squeezed into formulaic standards, they seem to be wrought with an emotion more generic than heartfelt.

Self-Congratulation

One theme that runs through all the speak-outs is self-congratulation—I have survived and now I am to be congratulated. Rhapsodies of self-affirmation may be part of "the healing practice," but as speaker after speaker praises herself for inner strength, they begin to seem excessive. From this spot in American culture, beneath Blair Arch at a Take Back the Night march, the population seems more oversaturated with self-esteem than with cholesterol. One common formulation at Take Back the Night is: "I am a survivor and it's a miracle every time I get a good grade, it's a miracle when I have friends, it's a miracle when I have relationships. It's a miracle. And I thank God every day." In the account in the *Daily Princetonian*, the survivor closes by saying, "If you don't know how to react next time you see me, give me a hug and tell me that you think I'm very brave. Because I, like all the other victims who speak out at Take Back the Night, am very brave."

In the context of Take Back the Night, it is entirely acceptable to praise yourself for bravery, to praise yourself for recovery, and to praise yourself for getting out of bed every morning and eating breakfast. Each story chronicles yet another ascent toward self-esteem, yet another "revolution from within."

As survivors tell their stories, as people hold hands, as they march and chant, there is undoubtedly a cathartic release. There is a current of support between listeners and speakers. At Columbia in 1992, students waited on line for hours to tell their stories, and as they did the listeners would chant, "It's not your fault," "We believe you," "We love you," and "Tell your story." The energy runs through the applause and the tears, the candlelight and the drumbeats. This is the same energy that sells millions of self-help books every year. This is march as therapy. . . .

A False Accusation

To be a part of this blanket warmth . . . , students are willing to lie. My first year at Princeton, one student was caught fabricating a rape story. Mindy had spoken at Take Back the Night for each of her four years at Princeton, and she had printed her story in the *Daily Princetonian*. What's interesting is that her account didn't really stand out; she sounded like everyone else at the speak-out. Her story could have been the blueprint. Whatever else anyone can say about her, Mindy could really talk the talk.

Her story went like this: she left the eating clubs after one boy "started hitting on me in a way that made me feel particularly uncomfortable." He followed her home and "dragged" her back to his room. The entire campus, as she described it, was indifferent: "Although I screamed the entire time, no one called for help, no one even looked out the window to see if the person screaming was in danger." He "carried" her to his room "and, while he shouted the most degrading obscenities imaginable, raped me." He told her that "his father buys him cheap girls like me to use up and throw away." And then he banged her head against the metal bedpost until she was unconscious. She then explained that he was forced to leave campus for a year and now he was back. "Because I see this person every day," she claimed, "my rape remains a constant daily reality for me." Now, she said, she was on the road to recovery, and "there are some nights when I sleep soundly and there are even some mornings when I look in the mirror and I like what I see. I may be a victim, but now I am also a survivor."

Unlike most participants in the speak-outs, Mindy put her story in print. Once it spilled over from the feverish midnight outpouring of the march into black-and-white newsprint, the facts could be checked. The problem was that she claimed she had reported a rape, and she hadn't. She claimed an administrator had told her "to let bygones be bygones," and he hadn't. She told people that a certain male undergraduate was the rapist, and he complained to the administration.

Political Fictions

In May of her senior year, 1991, Mindy came clean. Responding to administrative pressure, she printed an apology for her false accusation in the *Daily Princetonian*. She wrote of the person she accused, "I have never met this individual or spoken to him . . . I urge students who are knowledgeable of this situation to cease blaming this person for my attack." Mindy seemed to explain her motivation for inventing the story as political: "I made my statements in the *Daily Princetonian* and at the Take Back the Night March in order to raise awareness for the plight of the campus rape victims." So these were fictions in the service of political truth.

Mindy also claimed that she was swept up in the heat of the moment. "In several personal conversations and especially at the Take Back the Night March, I have been overcome by emotion. As a result, I was not as coherent or accurate in my recounting of events as a situation as delicate as this demands." If Mindy's political zeal and emotional intensity blurred the truth of her story, one wonders how many other survivors experience a similar blurring.

The accusation is a serious one, and the boy Mindy accused was in a terrible position in the community until she set the record straight. Accusations of rape stick, and in the twisted justice of the grapevine no one is considered innocent until proven guilty. Some may say, as an editorial in the *Daily Princetonian* did, that Mindy's false accusation was "an isolated incident" and shouldn't affect anyone's attitude toward Take Back the Night. Others would go further and claim that the abstract truth in these accusations eclipses the literal falsehood. In a piece about William Kennedy Smith's date-rape trial, Catharine MacKinnon, a prominent feminist law professor, wrote that the truth of a given accusation should be weighed in the larger political balance: "Did this member of a group sexually trained to woman-hating aggression commit this particular act of woman-hating aggression?" That people like MacKinnon are willing to sacrifice individual certainty to politicized group psychology only encourages the Mindys of the world to make up stories. . . .

The Spectacle of Mass Confession

The line between fact and fiction is a delicate one when it comes to survivor stories. In the heat of the moment, in the confessional rush of relating graphic details to a supportive crowd, the truth may be stretched, battered, or utterly abandoned. It's impossible to tell how many of these stories are authentic, faithful accounts of what actually happened. They all sound tinny, staged. Each "I am a survivor and I am here to take back the night" seems rehearsed. The context—microphone, hundreds of strangers, applause—puts what one survivor called "deepest darkest secrets" under a voyeuristic spotlight. As they listen to the stories, people cry and hold hands and put their arms around each other. The few moments before someone steps up to the microphone are thick with tension.

As students throw stories of suffering to the waiting crowds, the spiritual cleansing takes on darker undercurrents. The undercurrent is the competition for whose stories can be more Sadean, more incest-ridden, more violent, more like a paperback you can buy at a train station.

Under Blair Arch, a blind girl takes the microphone and says, I have been oppressed by everybody, straights and gays, Catholics, Jews and Protestants. Unless I am imagining it, a ripple of unease runs through the crowd. There is something obscene about this spectacle. This is theater, late-night drama. One earnest male Princeton junior tells me "it was better last year. More moving. There was more crying. Everyone was crying."

Some of these stories may be moving, may be heartfelt and true, but there is something about this context that numbs. Once, over a cup of coffee, a friend told me she had been raped by a stranger with a knife. I was startled. Small, neat, self-contained, she was not someone prone to bursts of self-revelation. She described it, the flash of the knife, the scramble, the exhaustion, the decision to keep her mind blank, the bruises and the police. After she had finished, she quickly resumed her competent, business-as-usual attitude, her toughness, but I could tell how hard it had been for her to tell me. I felt terrible for her. I felt like there was nothing I could say.

Victimhood Is Not Strength

But an individual conversation is worlds away from the spectacle of mass confession. I find the public demand—and it is a demand—for intimacy strange and unconvincing. Public confidences have a peculiarly aggressive quality. As Wendy Kaminer writes in her book about the recovery movement, "Never have so many known so much about people for whom they cared so little."

Besides the shady element of spectacle, the march itself is headed in the wrong direction. Take Back the Night works against its own political purpose. Although the march is intended to celebrate and bolster women's strength, it seems instead to celebrate their vulnerability. The marchers seem to accept, even embrace, the mantle of victim status. As the speakers describe every fear, every possible horror suffered at the hands of men, the image they project is one of helplessness and passivity. The march elaborates on just how vulnerable women are. Someone tells me that she wanted to say to the male speaker who said "This isn't . . . a good night to be a man" that it wasn't such a good night to be a woman either. *Drained, beleaguered, anxious,* and *vulnerable* are the words women use to describe how they feel as they walk away from the march. But there is a reason they come year after year. There is power to be drawn from declaring one's victimhood and oppression. There is strength in numbers, and unfortunately right now there is strength in being the most oppressed. Students scramble for that microphone, for a chance for a moment of authority. But I wonder if this kind of authority, the coat-tugging authority of the downtrodden, is really worth it.

Betty Friedan stirred up controversy with a bold critique of the rape-crisis movement. She attacked the political efficacy of this victimized and victimizing stance when she wrote, "Obsession with rape, even offering Band-Aids to its victims, is a kind of wallowing in that victim state, that impotent rage, that sterile polarization." *Impotent* and *sterile* are the right words. This is a dead-end gesture. Proclaiming victimhood doesn't help project strength.

> "*In most cases, the gist of memories is accurate; this statement is even more true of trauma memories.*"

Repressed Memories of Sexual Abuse Are Valid

James Lein

In the following viewpoint, James Lein responds to critics who contend that delayed recollections of childhood sexual abuse are often contrived. Contrary to claims that patients are motivated by their therapists to recall false memories of abuse, a victim's memories are more likely to be distorted by his or her abuser, in Lein's opinion. According to Lein, even if recovered memories of abuse contain some inaccuracies, most recollections are valid. In addition, he argues that recalling past abuse with the help of a therapist is crucial to an abuse victim's recovery. James Lein is a clinical social worker at the North Central Human Service Center in Minor, North Dakota.

As you read, consider the following questions:

1. What is the False Memory Syndrome Foundation, according to Lein?
2. As stated by the author, what happens when a patient undergoes a "cognitive shift"?
3. How does Lein's reference to World War II help support his argument that recovered memories are valid?

James Lein, "Recovered Memories: Context and Controversy," *Social Work*, vol. 44, September 1999, pp. 481–99. Copyright © 1999 by National Association of Social Workers, Inc. Reproduced by permission.

With the *Social Work* article "Recovered Memory Therapy: A Dubious Practice Technique" by J. T. Stocks (September 1998, pp. 423–436), *Social Work* has acknowledged, belatedly and obliquely, the controversy about trauma victims' recovered memories. I use the term "belatedly" because many professional publications, some with special editions, have, for several years now, focused directly on this extended and heated debate; for example, the *Harvard Mental Health Letter* (1993, 1994, 1995); almost all of the Winter 1995 *Journal of Psychohistory; Professional Psychology: Research and Practice* (October 1996); *American Psychologist* (September 1996, September 1997).

The False Memory Syndrome Foundation

I use the term "obliquely" because Stocks never outright mentioned the controversy and thus failed to place the *Social Work* article in context. Most obviously, Stocks neglected to mention the main protagonists in the recovered memory or false memory debate: Peter and Pamela Freyd and their daughter, Jennifer Freyd. In 1990 Jennifer, a psychologist, recalled childhood sexual abuse by her father, a mathematics professor. In response, her mother, an educator, founded in 1992 the False Memory Syndrome Foundation (FMSF), now with more than 18,000 members, people allegedly falsely accused of sexually abusing children. The foundation helps link alleged abusers with attorneys, who specialize in portraying therapists as false memory implanters, and with prominent scientist-experts, such as Elizabeth Loftus, who testify on the ease of implanting false memories of childhood trauma. Thus, a woman charging her father with molesting her as a child may face a well-orchestrated defense team, expert at discrediting her accusations and memories.

This is the context never mentioned in Stocks's (1998) article, which began: "Throughout most of this century, public response to sexual abuse of children had been to disregard, minimize, or deny allegations of child sexual abuse." In fact, the tactics of FMSF are a new and apparently scientific way of disregarding, minimizing, or denying allegations of child abuse. Not surprisingly, those accused of abuse, innocent or guilty, are likely to deny. Also, abusers, and not just victims, may have false memories; abusers certainly are strongly motivated to have false memories. They also are motivated to implant false memories in their victims. And they have considerable opportunity to influence or brainwash a child whom they may be with 24 hours a day by withholding or dispensing primary reinforcers, such as food or security. Compare this with a therapist working with an adult, an hour a week, withholding or dispensing secondary reinforcers, such as praise. Who has more power to implant so-called false memories? Who is more strongly motivated? Yes, some therapists may persuade some clients of abuse that never happened. But some perpetrators may persuade victims—as well as courts or researchers—that the abuse never happened. As L.J. Rubin has cautioned, perpetrator denial should not be denied:

> A balanced discussion must include consideration of explanations for forgetting episodes of perpetrating childhood sexual abuse, because accused perpetrators are certainly motivated not to admit abusive acts. . . . The longstanding denial of childhood sexual abuse harms society by permitting future victims. Denial harms perpetrators by ignoring the need and opportunity for treatment. . . . As psychologists, we must not perpetrate the denial of any aspect of sexual victimization.

The Nature of Memories

A very effective way of denying or muting charges of sexual abuse is to focus on so-called false memories. A very misleading term, false memory confuses two separate measures of memory: completeness and accuracy. As D. Brown et al. (1998) noted, a given memory may be incomplete yet highly accurate, as is often the case in young children's memory reports, or a given memory may be complete yet highly inaccurate. Is a memory false because it is not totally complete, down to tedious details, or because it contains inaccuracies? In most cases, the gist of memories is accurate; this statement is even more true of trauma memories. And as D. Spiegel and A.W. Scheftin (1994) observed: "It is illogical to reason from the fact that a memory has false details to the conclusion that there is no real incident from which this false memory is an inaccurate depiction. Even if a memory is shown to be inaccurate, this does not prove an event never happened." This, however, will probably sow sufficient doubt in a court of law to acquit an alleged child abuser—which, of course, is why such reasoning is used.

And it is relatively easy to create confusion and doubt about memories because they are indeed complicated and far from fully understood. In addition to the explicit memory–implicit memory distinction Stocks discussed, there are the semantic memory-episodic memory and the normal memory–traumatic memory distinctions. [Brown et al. write]: "According to accumulating neuro-biological data, normal, verbal autobiographical memories are primarily processed in the hippocampus, using a semantic categorizing processing system. . . . Traumatic memories are primarily processed in the limbic system, most likely in the amygdala."

KIDS WHO LIVE IN HELL

Rosen. © *Albany Times-Union*. Reprinted with permission.

Normal memory is more malleable and subject to constructivist distortion influences. Traumatic memories are more emotional and [according to J.E. LeDoux,] "are indelible and normally maintained by subcortical circuits involving

133

the amygdala," which is not part of the medial temporal lobe system involved with declarative or explicit memory, the system typically studied by false-memory researchers. Traumatic memory is also much more susceptible to fear conditioning. From an evolutionary perspective, this undoubtedly has survival value, triggering alarm reactions in situations that could lead to further abuse. However, these alarm reactions may become excessive, leaving victims, years later, depressed, anxious, and convinced that they are useless, vile, or deserving of nothing more than continued abuse. They may unintentionally drive away people who would be good partners and may accept abusers who give them what they think they deserve. These behaviors and thoughts are doubtless due in large part to abusers having told them as children either that what was occurring was not occurring—to forget it—or that they wanted it and deserved it.

The Importance of Remembering Abuse

In treating more than 150 adults who were sexually abused as children, I have seen their cognitive distortions [distorted thoughts] about self severely limit and handicap these otherwise capable people. Despite being aware of their own positive qualities and abilities and despite being very supportive of others, especially victims, these clients often experience a disconnect when it comes to concluding and knowing deep down that they, too, are worthwhile, deserving of love and support. To stop blaming and despising themselves, they seem to need some review and consideration of their abusive past—of how someone bigger and more powerful wronged them as a child. This cognitive shift, or reframing, seems to need some re-experiencing of oneself as a small, helpless person who was abused through no fault of one's own. Without some emotional and even painful reliving of the trauma, a client's talking about the abuse or about current problems usually fails to yield a positive shift in self-perception. In fact, [according to Brown et al.,] "what makes an emotionally charged experience integrative and most therapeutic is the accompanying cognitive-perceptual change that evolves after the catharsis." In working with these clients, individually and in groups, I have seen hardly any need to actively help them recover memories, although over half had experienced memory gaps. Most recovered some or all of their memories on their own, before coming in for therapy. In fact, this was one of their main symptoms: the intrusive memories crowding out their current life—with guilt, worthlessness, depression, desperation. Usually, when one's life is chaotic or in crisis, one does not have such intrusive memories; the chaos and crises tend to crowd them out. When a person's life is more stable and secure, these memories are more likely to surface. Sometimes this happens while the person is in therapy, where he or she may be more secure and where, perhaps for the first time, he or she is listened to. The vast majority of forgotten or dissociated memories recalled in therapy occur not because of active memory retrieval efforts but because of [as M. Price puts it,] "the creation of a context and a discourse that recognizes and acknowledges such traumas," a relationship in which it is safe to remember. "Free recall is how most good trauma treatment is conducted," [in the words of Brown et al.]

In good, state-of-the-art trauma treatment, according to Brown et al., memory recovery is always a subsidiary focus and never a primary goal of treatment. They agree with critics, like Stocks, that memory recovery techniques, if used inappropriately, apart from an integrated approach, are ill-advised. They disagree, though, with critics' assertions that recovered memory should never be a focus of treatment. Critic Stocks's article seems to suggest no way of helping clients deal with abuse memories other than assiduous avoidance of them. I have seldom seen it beneficial, however, for people to continue denying or living chaotic, memory-drowning lives. The costs are usually too high. But, of course, it is the client's call, whether to therapeutically face the past—and the possibility of being overwhelmed—or to numb it out one way or another. The therapist is available to help the client compare costs and open [what C.H. Cole and E.E. Barney term the] "therapeutic window," to find some balance between "denial phase symptoms" and "intrusive phase symptoms." But the therapist should not set the agenda, of either memory retrieval or memory avoidance. Perhaps more so than with any therapy, trauma treatment should carefully follow the client's lead.

More Light than Heat

Controversy, of course, continues over recovered memories, but, after a mainly contentious decade, the discussion finally seems to be generating more light than heat. Perhaps this is why *Social Work* delayed joining in. Whatever the reason, it is good that an additional forum has opened up for social workers, who undoubtedly treat the majority of abuse victims—children and adults.

In conclusion, I recommend, as part of this memory recovery discussion, the 786-page book by Brown et al. [entitled *Memory, Trauma Treatment, and the Law*] and the three-page article by B.P. Karon and A.J. Widener (1997) [entitled "Repressed Memories and World War II: Last We Forget!"], who found "it astounding that so many authoritative statements by contemporary psychologists and psychiatrists refer to repression and repressed memories as a myth" when, in World War II, there were hundreds of documented cases of recovered traumatic combat experiences, usually with eyewitness observers of the event forgotten only by the amnesic victim. Karon and Widener concluded their brief article:

> The war neuroses of WWII provide ample evidence that . . . the recovery of these traumatic memories and their related effects led to remission of symptoms. Moreover, these recovered memories were of events that had unquestionably occurred. Current controversies concerning repressed memories are always discussed without reference to this well-documented body of data, which was well-known at the time but seems to have been forgotten. The mental health professions, just as individual patients, need to remember their past in order to be effective in the real world.

"Brain-imaging studies show memory and imagination involve the same areas of the cerebral cortex—it is hard to separate the two."

Repressed Memories of Sexual Abuse Are a Hoax

Rael Jean Isaac

Rael Jean Isaac contends in the following viewpoint that feminists have exaggerated the extent of child sexual abuse by popularizing the notion that victims can recall repressed memories of abuse during therapy. According to Isaac, most recovered memories are too absurd to be believed and have probably been created by the imagination. In addition, Isaac maintains, studies alleging to prove the validity of recovered memories are seriously flawed. Rael Jean Isaac is coauthor of the book *Madness in the Streets: How Psychiatry and the Law Abandoned the Mentally Ill.*

As you read, consider the following questions:

1. What are two of the questions that Ellen Bass and Laura Davis ask in their book *The Courage to Heal*, according to Isaac?
2. As stated by the author, what type of memories are the least likely to be forgotten?
3. What did abuse victim Nadean Cool remember during therapy, according to the author?

Rael Jean Isaac, "Sex, Lies, and Audiotapes," *Women's Quarterly*, Summer 2001, p. 7. Copyright © 2001 by *Women's Quarterly*. Reproduced by permission.

There is a widespread belief that sexual abuse of children is endemic to society. This is a relatively new notion. In fact, it can be traced to a particular moment in history: April 17, 1971.

The Roots of False Memory Syndrome

On that day the New York Radical Feminists, a group that at its height boasted no more than 400 members, held a groundbreaking conference on rape in New York. For two days, women held forth on a subject long considered taboo. Susan Brownmiller, who would go on to write *Against Our Will*, a classic in the literature of rape, later described a speech given by Florence Rush as the highlight of the event.

"I have been to many feminist meetings," Brownmiller recalled, "but never before, and not since, have I seen an entire audience rise to its feet in acclaim. We clapped. We cheered."

Rush was an unlikely star for such a gathering. A middle-aged social worker, who had never been raped, she outlined statistical studies suggesting that sexual abuse of children, including incest, was a more widespread problem than was generally recognized. It was Rush's conclusion that electrified her audience: "The family itself is an instrument of sexual and other forms of child abuse," Rush declared. She added that this abuse "is permitted because it is an unspoken but prominent factor in socializing and preparing the female to accept a subordinate role. . . . In short the sexual abuse of female children is a process of education that prepares them to become the wives and mothers of America."

The Great American Secret

Many women at the gathering had backgrounds in the New Left of the 1960s. They felt their male comrades had exploited them, relegating them to making coffee, typing, and sex.

Now they could show that feminists had uncovered the great American secret: Behind the picket fences, hidden by those starched suburban curtains, fathers were raping daughters to prepare them for their proper role in society. Beyond racism, imperialism, and capitalism lay the true root of evil—patriarchy.

Before Rush's speech, feminists had given little thought to incest. Author Andrea Dworkin recalled that before the conference "we never had any idea how common it was." In the decades following Rush's talk, feminists more than made up for their earlier unawareness, competing with each other in elevating the number of victims.

Catharine MacKinnon, the law professor who helped develop the legal definitions of sexual harassment, announced (absent any evidence) that 4.5 percent of all women are victims of incest by their fathers and, if brothers, stepfathers, uncles, and family friends are thrown in, the figure rose to 40 percent. "In fact," wrote MacKinnon, "it is the woman who has not been sexually abused who deviates." Seemingly scholarly studies by feminists-with-credentials such as Harvard psychiatrist Judith Herman bolstered the case for widespread incest. Herman dedicated her 1981 book, *Father-Daughter Incest*, to the women "estimated by us to be in the millions, who have personally experienced incestuous abuse." No wonder Andrea Dworkin wrote that, for a woman, the home is the most dangerous place in the world!

As the feminists saw it, bringing incestuous rape out of the closet would finally vindicate the truth of women's experience. Sigmund Freud, the father of modern psychotherapy, had believed early in his career that sexual abuse was the cause of his female patients' neurotic symptoms. Later, however, Freud dismissed such testimony from his female patients as fantasy. According to Herman, "Freud simply could not confront the reality that incest is an inevitable result of patriarchal family structure."

Believe the Women

Believe the women. Believe the children. These refrains became the mantra of the incest movement. While the women's movement would be enormously successful in turning sexual abuse—including incest—into a major public issue, women, ironically, would become the chief victims of the hysteria it generated.

The obsession with this supposedly rampant sexual abuse played out in [damaging ways]: "Believe the women" became the repressed memory hysteria. . . .

At the time of the conference, psychiatric textbooks esti-mated the rate of father-daughter incest at one to two for ev-ery million women in the United States. If that figure was ac-curate, it was not surprising that incest attracted little public attention. On the other hand, if, in fact, fathers were sexually abusing millions of daughters, why did no one know of it?

Hypnosis Is an Unreliable Memory Recovery Method

Although hypnosis can increase the amount of information and vividness of recall, such information occurs for accurate as well as inaccurate recall. There are many examples of in-dividuals confidently reporting hypnotically induced false memories as real ones. These studies demonstrating the lim-itations of hypnotic memory recovery led the Council on Scientific Affairs of the American Medical Association (1986) to conduct a study of recall during hypnosis. The council re-ported that such recollections were often less reliable than nonhypnotic recall. Subsequent research has supported the findings that hypnosis is an unreliable memory recovery method.

J.T. Stocks, "Recovered Memory Therapy: A Dubious Practice," *Social Work*, September 1998.

The theory of "repressed memory" provided the answer. A woman was so traumatized by being molested by her father, the theory said, that she banished the memory from her con-scious mind. Paul McHugh, head of the Department of Psy-chiatry at Johns Hopkins Medical School, is skeptical of re-pressed memory. McHugh sees the development of the concept as one of the "misadventures" of the last thirty years that show "the power of cultural fashion to lead psychiatric thought and practice off in false, even disastrous, directions."

Poorly Grounded in Science

However poorly grounded in science, the theory helped ex-plain why so few women remembered their incestuous expe-riences until they entered therapy. According to the theory, the intact, repressed memory festered in a special part of the brain producing, as psychiatrist Lenore Terr put it, "signs and symptoms" that disrupted the woman's life. While Terr and

Herman were important in lending a cloak of medical legitimacy to the idea of repressed memory, the most influential work was *The Courage to Heal: A Guide for Women Survivors of Child Sexual Abuse* by Ellen Bass and Laura Davis, neither of whom had training in psychiatry. Published in 1988, *The Courage to Heal* has sold more than 700,000 copies.

The book asked such questions as: Do you have difficulty expressing your feelings? Problems trusting your intuition? Have an eating disorder? Feel different from other people? Feel powerless, like a victim? If you answered "yes" to these or exhibited any of a host of other "symptoms," *The Courage to Heal* said that it was time to consider the possibility that you had been sexually abused as a child.

Convinced sexual abuse was endemic and seeing such symptoms as "evidence," therapists of all types, from psychiatrists on down, set out to "help" patients unlock their buried memories. They used a variety of methods, including hypnosis, injections of sodium amytal ("truth serum"), guided imagery, dream work, participation in survivor groups, even massage therapy to recover "body memories" of abuse. Yet as social psychology professor Richard Ofshe points out in *Making Monsters*, the scientific grounding for all this was absent.

The Nature of Memory

Indeed, studies on memory show that intense emotional experiences are the least likely to be forgotten. Ironically, Dr. Terr's reputation was based on her study of twenty-six children who had been kidnapped from a school bus in Chowchilla, California, and entombed in a truck trailer. She found that years after the traumatic experience each child retained detailed memories of the event. Nor is there any evidence that traumatic memories are stored in pristine form in a special part of the brain. On the contrary, as forensic psychologist Dr. Terence Campbell points out, brain-imaging studies show memory and imagination involve the same areas of the cerebral cortex—it is hard to separate the two.

As for hypnosis (and sodium amytal), the American Medical Association's Council on Scientific Affairs states: "Contrary to what is generally believed by the public, recollections obtained during hypnosis not only fail to be more accurate but actually appear to be generally less reliable than nonhypnotic recall." The American Psychiatric Association guidelines note that "no specific unique symptom profile has been identified that necessarily correlated with abuse experiences."

Mothers and Fathers

While feminists always assumed the abuser was male, Florence Rush found in her work with (genuinely) abused children that these young victims frequently focused their rage on their mothers. Rush argued that it is men, not women, who actually rape our young and it is time for them, not women, to be held responsible. Or, as feminist writer Robin Morgan succinctly put it, "Kill your father, not your mother." Still, a 1993 survey of over a thousand cases by the False Memory Syndrome Foundation, the Philadelphia-based organization that has been in the forefront of exposing problems with recovered memory therapy, found that in fully a third of cases, the mother was accused of active sexual abuse.

Even those daughters who identified their fathers as the abuser blamed their mothers for failing to protect them. Some remembered the mothers' holding them down while their fathers raped them. That is what Beth Rutherford claimed happened. Rutherford, after two years in therapy, "remembered" her minister-father twice impregnating her and then performing a coat-hanger abortion (never mind that a medical examination showed she was a virgin). Rutherford convinced her sisters that they were also in danger of being murdered by their father. One sister actually went into hiding, and all three cut off any communication with both parents. Beth Rutherford has since recanted the accusations and written about her family's ordeal.

Satanic Ritual Abuse Allegations

While it may be hard to summon up much sympathy for the daughter who rips apart her family because of therapist-induced delusions, in many cases she is clearly the biggest victim of all. As therapy proceeds, she produces ever more lurid memories. Indeed, in an estimated 15 percent of cases, the repressed memory patient develops memories of satanic ritual abuse. Increasingly satanic cult survivors are realizing they were victims of their therapists and are suing them for malpractice. The evidence of therapist misconduct is so impressive, and jury verdicts have been so high that many insurance companies now settle during the trial.

Dr. Bennett Braun's insurance company settled for $10.6 million the day his trial was to begin. Dr. Braun's patient, Patricia Burgus, had, through therapy, become convinced that she had been the high priestess of a satanic cult. Hospitalized for over two years, Burgus "remembered" lit torches pushed inside her and having to eat body parts of 2,000 people in one year.

While under the care of Dr. Kenneth Olson, Nadean Cool became convinced that she had 120 personalities (including that of a duck), had knifed babies in the heart and passed them around to other cult members to eat. . . . In the Cool case, the insurance company settled for $2.4 million after fifteen days of testimony. . . .

Shattered Lives

As for the women with "repressed memories" who cut themselves off from their parents, even going so far as to sue them in civil or criminal court, many have recanted their accusations or reestablished ties without saying they were wrong. Many families remain permanently estranged. . . . But the lives of all those involved were shattered, and it is hard to put Humpty Dumpty together again.

The feminists who rallied around Florence Rush believed that they could end child abuse by abolishing the patriarchal family, which was its "cause." Instead they launched a child abuse hysteria in which pseudo-science has flourished. Both men and women have been its victims.

"It is [now] possible for a woman to defend herself in her own home by killing her attacker."

Battered Woman Syndrome Is a Valid Defense

Douglas A. Orr

Battered woman syndrome has been used as a defense by women who claim that killing their husbands was the only way they could escape spousal abuse. In the following viewpoint, Douglas A. Orr asserts that the battered woman syndrome defense has benefited abused women who have too often been revictimized by the law, which has a tendency to disadvantage women. He praises the 1999 Florida *Weiand v. State* case for establishing that battered women are legally entitled to defend themselves in their own homes against abusive husbands. Douglas A. Orr is an attorney admitted to practice in Florida and New Jersey. He earned his B.A. at Seton Hall University, an M.A. in English at Rutgers University, and his J.D. at Rutgers School of Law in Newark.

As you read, consider the following questions:
1. As stated by Orr, what are the three phases in the battered spouse syndrome cycle?
2. What three elements must be present to justify homicide under any claim of self-defense, according to the author?
3. As reported by Orr, what percentage of men who kill their female partners use a weapon other than their fists?

Douglas A. Orr, "*Weiand v. State* and Battered Spouse Syndrome," *Florida Bar Journal*, vol. 74, June 2000, p. 14. Copyright © 2000 by *Florida Bar Journal*. Reproduced by permission.

In March 1999, Florida's Supreme Court effectively granted Florida women the ability to rely upon battered spouse syndrome as a defense to killing their abuser. Prior to the court's 1999 decision in *Weiand v. State*, an abused woman's ability to justifiably defend herself from a physically abusive husband or live-in boyfriend was no greater than that of anyone to defend themselves in a bar fight. Although *Weiand* has wide-reaching implications for any person attacked in his or her home, the unfortunate reality is that women who are attacked by paramours are most likely to be the ultimate beneficiaries of the *Weiand* holding. Previously, Florida followed the minority rule among states, which imposes a duty to retreat before defending oneself with deadly force. Courts did recognize the limited "castle doctrine" exception, which provides that there is no duty to retreat when attacked in one's own home. However, prior to *Weiand*, a gray area existed: What if both assailant and victim lived in that house? Was there a duty to retreat, or could a battered woman rely upon the castle doctrine, stand her ground, and defend herself with deadly force? The law was unsettled. The *Weiand* decision answers this question.

The *Weiand* Case

Kathleen Weiand shot and killed her husband Todd. At trial, Kathleen's defense was battered spouse syndrome; she lived in such fear of Todd that she had no choice but to kill him, fearing that if she did not, he would kill her. Defense expert Dr. Lenore Walker, a clinical and forensic psychologist, testified that Kathleen showed all the signs of battered spouse syndrome and that she believed Todd was going to kill her. However, the court's jury instruction included the admonition that "[t]he fact that the defendant was wrongfully attacked cannot justify her use of force likely to cause death or great bodily harm if by retreating she could have avoided the need to use that force." One year after Kathleen pulled the trigger, an eight-woman, four-man jury rejected the battered spouse syndrome defense and convicted Kathleen Weiand of second degree murder for killing Todd. Approximately one month later, Kathleen Weiand was sentenced to 18 years in prison. Florida's Second District Court of Appeal would affirm her conviction. However, because the Florida Supreme Court considered the issue to be of great public importance, *Weiand v. State* was reargued.

Abused women who live in fear for their lives and who ultimately kill their abuser may suffer from battered spouse syndrome. Battered spouse syndrome is created by a cycle of physical abuse within a relationship. Typically, there are three phases in a cycle. Phase one involves minor battering incidents, verbal abuse, and attempts by the woman to placate the man. Phase two involves an "acute battering incident" where the woman is severely beaten. Phase three is one of contrition and loving behavior on the part of the male, which reinforces the woman's hope for her mate's reform. Some time later, phase one begins again. The cumulative effect of this cycle of abuse is that the woman becomes perpetually fearful of the man and feels helpless to improve her situation. Killing her abuser becomes her only escape from the relationship. . . .

The Tripartite Self-Defense Standard

To justify homicide under any claim of self-defense, a defendant must establish the presence of three elements: 1) the defendant believed she must use force against an imminent threat of harm; 2) the amount of force used was proportionate to the threatened harm; and 3) the defendant retreated to the greatest degree reasonably possible. Evidence that a woman suffers from battered spouse syndrome addresses part one of this standard, namely, whether the woman honestly feared for her life.

Part three of this tripartite self-defense standard, the duty to retreat, is inapplicable in a defendant's own home because of the so-called "castle doctrine," or privilege of nonretreat. The castle doctrine provides that if an assailant threatens a victim with violence in the victim's own home, the victim may turn aggressor without any duty of retreat, and still be able to justify his actions by claiming self-defense.

This theory is premised on the notion that "a man's home is his castle," hence the name "castle doctrine." Justice Cardozo explained, "It is not now and never has been the law that a man assailed in his own dwelling is bound to retreat. If assailed there, he may stand his ground and resist the attack. He is under no duty to take to the fields and the highways, a fugitive from his own home." Florida, and most other states, has adopted the castle doctrine exception to self-defense's duty to retreat. Yet, the castle doctrine is not absolute.

The *Bobbitt* Case

Complications arise when both initial attacker/ultimate victim and the initial victim/ultimate killer live in the same home. Under the castle doctrine's rationale, both parties have an equal right to defend themselves against an attack. In 1982, the Florida Supreme Court, in *State v. Bobbitt*, held that the castle doctrine does not apply where both a criminal defendant and his victim are legal occupants of the same home and have equal rights to be there. In that situation, a victim's duty to retreat remains intact. In *Bobbitt*, the defendant shot and killed her husband, who attacked her in their home without provocation. The *Bobbitt* court grounded its decision on the sanctity of property and possessory rights. Neither victim nor slayer has a greater right than the other to stand his ground and defend against an attack. . . .

The court decided to overrule *Bobbitt* because of its implications for victims of domestic violence. The court's concern was that imposing a duty to retreat from the home would adversely impact victims of domestic violence. Citing studies and articles that suggest women who back off or away from violent confrontations do more to perpetuate their cycle of violence and victimization than to break it, the court concluded that forcing women to walk away from their abuser may actually increase the threat to their lives, not minimize it. Most pointedly, the court cited a Florida Governor's Task Force on Domestic Violence report that states, "forty-five percent of the murders of women were generated by the man's rage over the actual or impending estrangement from his partner." The court concludes this argument by stating that retaining a duty to retreat from the home handicaps women and wives from defending themselves against an aggressor spouse.

The court's other concern was that a jury instruction on the duty to retreat would reinforce, legitimize, and strengthen myths and stereotypes about domestic violence. One of the most pervasive myths surrounding domestic violence is that women may leave an abusive situation whenever they want. In Kathleen Weiand's case, this myth was almost certainly perpetuated. Her jury's instruction included the duty to retreat, a fact the prosecutor capitalized on when he highlighted the fact that Kathleen did not leave the house or get in her car before picking up a gun. The court feels . . . that expert testimony on a battered woman's feelings of helplessness is relevant to the jury's understanding of the legitimacy of a battered woman's feelings of imminent harm. To permit a jury instruction that suggests retreat is an option for a battered woman would completely undermine that expert's testimony. . . .

Horsey. © 1999 *Seattle Post-Intelligencer*. Reprinted by permission of North American Syndicate.

The remaining issue for the court, then, is what jury instruction should be given in cases of domestic violence slayings where the defendant claims self-defense? Although the court points to no studies that suggest a privilege of nonretreat could result in an increase of domestic violence incidents and homicides, the court is concerned that completely eliminating a duty to retreat might invite violence. For this reason, the court adopted a jury instruction that "imposes a limited duty to retreat within the residence to the extent reasonably possible, but not to flee the residence." . . .

The Equal Force Doctrine

The Weiand case only resolves part three of the self-defense standard: the duty to retreat. Judicial recognition of the validity of battered spouse syndrome resolves part one of the test; the reasonableness of a defendant's belief that harm was imminent. However, part two of the test, that the amount of force used must proportionate to the threatened harm, leaves most beaten women unable to adequately defend themselves, and completely unable to claim self-defense at trial. When attacked by a man, women, on the whole, lack the ability to respond proportionately to the harm he is inflicting upon her. Thus, women are at a fundamental disadvantage to claim self-defense because they cannot respond to an attack with equal force.

Approximately one-fourth of all murders committed in the United States stem from family battles. Over 50 percent of all murders occur between conjugal partners. Furthermore, while men and women are about equally responsible for killing their spouses, wives are more than seven times as likely to kill as a last resort, in self-defense. The overwhelming majority of battering victims are women. Given these and other startling facts, it becomes clear that domestic abuse is an enormous problem in America.

Many women who kill their abusers are convicted of murder because of an inherent flaw in the law of self-defense that stems from the law being written, and enforced, by men. A feminist perspective on the law of self-defense should gain wider support and would address this fundamental inequality.

Because men wrote the law of self-defense, the law has a tendency to disadvantage women. Based on the prototypical combat situation, with two men of roughly equal size and strength, the doctrine of equal force makes sense: If attacked by a man without a deadly weapon, another man may not justifiably defend himself with a deadly weapon. That would not be self-defense with equal force. The doctrine of equal force evolved because the male defendant has a wide range of weapons and abilities from which he can select a degree of force proportionate to that of his attacker and adequate to defend himself. However, because women are generally physically smaller and weaker than men, the equal force requirement is impractical in the context of domestic abuse and self-defense. "This rule ignores the woman who reasonably feels unable to protect herself without a deadly weapon, even though her husband-assailant is unarmed," [as stated by Michael A. Budd and Teresa L. Butler].

A woman who is being beaten by her husband, who is using fists and kicks to inflict non-life-threatening injuries upon her, cannot respond with equal force. She lacks the strength that is necessary to counterbalance the harm that a man is able to inflict on her. So, she grabs the next best thing—a gun—and shoots him. Responding to his abuse with proportionate force is not an option for her, so she must rely on the next best thing—a greater force.

The Need for Weapons

Most battered women who kill their abusers must resort to a weapon. Out of 100 abused women who killed their assailants, 75 used a gun, knives were used 13 times, five women used a car, one a sledgehammer, one poison, one fire and the final four hired killers. In contrast, only three quarters of men who kill their female partners use any weapon other than their fists. Florida's law of self-defense must address this biological inequity that exists in our equal force doctrine.

The courts of other states have attempted to resolve the equal force doctrine by permitting a woman to use a weapon against an unarmed attacker. These states allow an attacked woman to strike back with force that is proportional and reasonable, not identical. But Florida courts have not addressed this problem with the equal force doctrine. In this respect, Florida courts must move toward the position held by the majority in this country. Perhaps in recognition of the inadequacy of this state's self-defense laws to battered women, between 1992 and 1999, 23 Florida women who were imprisoned for killing their fathers, spouses, or boyfriends have been granted clemency.

Most importantly, after *Weiand v. State*, it is possible for a woman to defend herself in her own home by killing her attacker—any attacker. By removing the absolute duty to retreat, battered spouse syndrome now has legal "teeth" in Florida. The next step will be for the court to recognize the practical impossibility that the equal force doctrine is to most women and remove that weapon from the hands of their attackers.

> *"Battered woman syndrome appears to be the product of legal advocacy and not science."*

Battered Woman Syndrome Is Not a Valid Defense

Joe Wheeler Dixon

Battered woman syndrome is the psychological state suffered by women who fear that they will be killed by their abusive husbands if they try to leave the relationship. Joe Wheeler Dixon explains in the following viewpoint that battered woman syndrome has been used in many court cases to absolve women for killing their husbands. However, according to Dixon, the syndrome has no scientific basis. In fact, it is impossible to tell who suffers from the syndrome because the signs that clinicians use to diagnose it can be found in numerous conditions, Dixon points out. Moreover, he asserts that the use of battered woman syndrome in court cases actually harms women by perpetuating stereotypes of female helplessness and mental deficiency. Joe Wheeler Dixon is a clinical and forensic psychologist and an adjunct professor of law at Cumberland School of Law at Samford University in Birmingham, Alabama.

As you read, consider the following questions:
1. According to Dixon, what clinical trap compromises diagnoses of battered woman syndrome?
2. What are some of the unintended consequences of using battered woman syndrome as a legal defense, in the author's view?

Joe Wheeler Dixon, "Battered Woman Syndrome," www.expertlaw.com, January 2002. Copyright © 2002 by ExpertLaw. Reproduced by permission of the author.

B attered woman syndrome (BWS) was first proposed in the 1970's and was essentially based on the clinical observations of a single researcher. Nevertheless, the concept quickly caught on and became a popular way to justify behavior in some courts. However, while it initially enjoyed success in portions of the legal arena, BWS has not been established nor accepted in the field of psychology by serious and rigorous empirical researchers.

No Evidence for BWS

To be sure, clinical syndromes do exist, and BWS may indeed exist, but to date there is insufficient empirical evidence to show this syndrome meets the rigorous diagnostic criteria of psychology or the law. If BWS does exist, there is no reliable means to identify those who suffer from it from those who merely claim it as a legal defense.

BWS appears to be the product of legal advocacy and not science. BWS seems to owe its existence to the needs of legal advocates to support and justify claims by battered women who have killed. Given the lack of an established, empirical, scientific basis and its failure to achieve specific political and social policy goals for women, BWS may not be long for this world.

BWS has been employed in a wide assortment of cases, ranging from the prototypical self-defense case to the more novel prosecutorial use of the syndrome. In the former set of cases, courts define the syndrome's relevance variously, from supporting the honesty of the woman's belief in the need to use deadly force to her mental incapacity to form the requisite mental intent. In the latter set of cases, in which prosecutors use the evidence, the evidence's relevance is ostensibly offered to explain why a battered woman might change her testimony (i.e., commit perjury) and testify that she was not a victim of battering; in fact, BWS is probably used to buttress the prosecution's case by showing prior violent acts by the defendant that would otherwise be excluded by the rules of evidence.

The Trap

BWS offers broad interpretations of conduct for which there is no empirical support. As courts begin to apply *Daubert* styled tests of admissibility [named after the 1993 U.S. Supreme Court decision in which the rules for the admission of expert testimony were changed] that query the scientific basis for BWS testimony, they will discover the serious lack of scientific support for BWS. There are numerous non-specific signs that a clinician favorably biased towards BWS will "see" in the reports of a woman relating a history of battering. Such clinicians are quick to then label the clinical history as causing BWS, and the BWS as justifying or explaining the woman's subsequent unlawful conduct. The clinical error or trap lies in the fact that these signs are commonly seen in a variety of conditions, and none are specifically tied to BWS. Further, the patient can simply lie about or exaggerate their abusive history with a host of non-specific signs. There is a human tendency to accept ready explanations and BWS offers just that. This unreliable manner leads to inaccurate diagnosis. A principal tenet of science is there must first be reliability, and absent this, there can be no validity, that is, no trustworthy diagnosis. So, how can anyone determine who does and who does not suffer with BWS? The simple answer is, we cannot.

Advocates for battered women with a social agenda should begin in the near future to doubt the political value of BWS testimony. Although so elastic that it can be shaped to fit any legal case, the syndrome per se has caused certain unintended consequences. In particular, BWS evidence is interpreted by many courts as an indication that battered women suffer from mental deficiencies. Judges may doubt the veracity or accuracy of a defendant claiming the syndrome. For instance, courts are increasingly ordering women claiming the defense to undergo psychological evaluations. Originally proposed as a theory entirely sympathetic to feminist ideals, the syndrome now reinforces some of the most archaic and destructive stereotypes historically attached to women.

Lawyers and judges are obliged to become better consumers of science. Too much is at stake for them to fail in this. BWS originally tapped into a reservoir of disenchantment, frustration, and sometimes outrage over domestic violence. Domestic violence in our country is very real, and according to some reports, it is of epidemic proportions.

Absolving Women of Responsibility

The Battered Woman Syndrome ought not to be seen as a way to absolve a woman of responsibility for her actions. Yet juries often understand BWS as mental incapacity. As author of the book *Battered Women Who Kill* Charles Ewing points out, if the jury believes a woman suffers from a mental incapacity, then she cannot be considered as acting in a reasonable manner, which is what is required by the self-defense standard. If a woman who kills her batterer in self-defense is seen as not responsible for her actions because of a mental incapacity (BWS), then she continues to exist in an invisible moral realm wherein she is not perceived as exercising or capable of exercising full moral personhood.

Sally J. Scholz, "Moral Implications of the Battered Woman Syndrome," www.bu.edu.

Keying on this information and widespread sentiments, BWS in the guise of science accomplished a small revolution in the way battered women cases were seen by courts and the public. Using the cloak of science to avoid the difficult jurisprudential questions raised when battered women kill, advocates of BWS found initial success and notoriety. However, today and in the future, these advocates may likely find themselves in the same old world, possibly worse off than before. In fact, there may have been harm done to the reputation of the science of psychology because of the well intended but poorly grounded efforts of just a handful of clinicians.

Learned Helplessness

The syndrome has become a psychological-styled diagnosis in which the woman's "illness," induced by a battering husband, has become the focus. The focus might better remain on the woman herself with traditional legal defenses proffered, such as self-defense. The creation of a syndrome per se is of little help in stemming the tide of battering and domestic violence. The BWS defense now revolves around the woman's mental deficiency and, paradoxically, her purported helplessness. Learned helplessness can be induced in laboratory animals, but with laboratory animals we do not observe a sudden rousing of rage and aggression at any point in the course of their condition. Thus, BWS does not follow the known course of experimentally induced helplessness syndromes. BWS is an anomaly. It does not exist in the laboratory, and it may well not exist in the real world.

History reveals several examples of well meaning clinicians incorrectly applying scientific research to explaining the clinical suffering observed in their patients. BWS is of course one such example. As a point of comparison, another such syndrome is repressed memory syndrome (RMS). This syndrome alleges that young women who were sexually abused as children by their fathers repress the memory of these traumatic events, but they later suffer depression and other psychological disorders. Again, scientific research disputes RMS, because what empirical studies find is that traumatic events, such as being raped, are highlighted and magnified in the memories of victims, not repressed. In fact, these victims obsess and dwell upon these memories and it is the constant recall, not suppression, of these events which lead to depression, anxiety, and other psychological symptoms.

As courts begin to realize that BWS expert testimony lacks a scientific, or even a reliable technical basis, and women advocates realize that this testimony is inimical to their cause, the battered woman syndrome should begin to fall into disuse. As it leaves the legal and clinical scene, advocates of battered women and proponents of good science should join efforts to discover solutions to the domestic battering that occurs in our country. Women who kill should be treated by the courts with the existing laws that have served us well for so long.

Periodical Bibliography

The following articles have been selected to supplement the diverse views presented in this chapter.

Anonymous "The Day My Life Changed," *British Medical Journal*, October 28, 2000.

Elizabeth Ashley and Doris Bacon "Rape and Denial: An Attack on a Friend Caused Me to Confront a Sexual Assault I'd Tried to Block from My Mind for 16 Years," *People Weekly*, August 16, 1993.

C.J. Carnacchio "'Take Back the Night'—No Men Allowed," *Michigan Review*, April 21, 1999. www.umich.edu.

Patricia Gaddis "In the Beginning . . . A Creation Story of Battered Women's Shelters," *Off Our Backs*, October 2001.

Joseph Hallinan "'Repressed Memory' or Fake Flashbacks?" *Washington Times*, December 26, 1996.

Donna Laframboise "Battered Shelters: Criminal Charges, Mismanagement, Infighting, and Sexual Politics Have Left Many Women's Shelters as Bruised as the People They Serve," *National Post*, November 14, 1998.

Harrison G. Pope Jr. "Recovered Memories of Childhood Sexual Abuse: The Royal College of Psychiatrists Issues Important Precautions," *British Medical Journal*, February 14, 1998.

Lori S. Rubenstein "What Is Battered Woman's Syndrome?" www.divorcenet.com.

Sally J. Scholz "Moral Implications of the Battered Woman Syndrome." www.bu.edu.

J.T. Stocks "Recovered Memory Therapy: A Dubious Practice Technique," *Social Work*, September 1998.

Suzannne Stutman "Take Back the Night Address." www.feminist.com.

Joy S. Taylor "No Shelter from the Storm," *Liberty*, July 1997.

Walter Williams "'Battered Woman Syndrome' or Battered Truth Syndrome?" *Capitalism Magazine*, April 12, 2002. www.capitalismmagazine.com.

CHAPTER 4

How Can Sexual Violence Be Reduced?

Chapter Preface

On a cold February night in 1999, sisters Leclair and Corrine McKeowen called 911 five times to report that one of the sisters' ex-boyfriend was breaching a restraining order. Both women were found stabbed to death in their Canadian home shortly after their last call.

Many analysts point to the McKeowen case as evidence that laws designed to protect women from violence are inadequate. Restraining orders, they point out, are just pieces of paper. Taking the abuser to court may get him locked away for a while, but he will eventually get out. Alternative solutions such as relocating are not foolproof either. Not only does the woman have to give up her job, her home, and her social support group, but moving away does not guarantee that her abuser will not find her. Besides, if the woman and her abuser have children together, the court may require joint custody, making relocation impossible. In light of these difficulties, many commentators have proposed a controversial solution: Women should arm themselves.

Many experts maintain that women are victims of violence and sexual abuse more often than are men for the simple fact that men are bigger, stronger, and more aggressive than are women. Conservative columnist Ann Coulter contends that "guns are [women's] friends, because in a world without guns I'm what is known as prey. Almost all females are. Any male—even the sickliest 98-pound weakling—could overpower me in a contest of brute force against brute force." Coulter adds, "we can't have a world without violence, because the world is half male and testosterone causes homicide. A world with violence—that is to say, with men—but without weapons is the worst of all possible worlds for women." Researcher John Lott Jr. reports that women who are armed fare better during attempted rapes than women who are unarmed. According to Lott, if an unarmed woman resists an attack, she is 2.5 times more likely to be harmed or killed than a resisting woman who is armed.

Despite some people's belief that guns are an effective way to reduce violence against women, many women remain resistant to the idea. Canadian attorney Karen Selick reports that abused women recoil when she suggests that they arm themselves. According to Selick, her clients say, "I'd be afraid to own a gun. I'll just call the police if he shows up." However, as the McKeowen case illustrates, sometimes calling 911 is not enough. The authors in the following chapter debate several controversial strategies for reducing sexual violence and protecting victims. To be sure, such proposals can have profound consequences for victims like Leclair and Corrine McKeowen.

> *"Chemical castration legislation could provide one more alternative to ease the problem of recidivism in certain populations of sex offenders."*

Chemical Castration Can Help Reduce Sexual Violence

Christopher Meisenkothen

Chemical castration refers to the use of the birth control drug Depo Provera to curb the sexual appetites of some types of sex offenders. In the following viewpoint, Christopher Meisenkothen argues that chemically castrating sex offenders released on probation would help them control their unnatural sexual urges and protect society. He contends that the use of Depo Provera does not violate the constitutional protection against cruel and unusual punishment because chemical castration is a treatment, not a punishment. Moreover, charges that chemical castration would violate the constitutionally protected right to refuse treatment are unfounded because sex offenders have a choice whether to undergo the treatment or remain in prison, he asserts. Christopher Meisenkothen is an attorney practicing in New Haven, Connecticut.

As you read, consider the following questions:
1. As defined by Meisenkothen, what is a paraphiliac?
2. What examples does the author provide to illustrate his point that no fundamental right is absolute?
3. Why does chemical castration fail to violate the right to procreate, according to the author?

Christopher Meisenkothen, "Chemical Castration—Breaking the Cycle of Paraphiliac Recidivism," *Social Justice*, vol. 26, Spring 1999, pp. 139–54. Reproduced by permission.

Chemical castration. The words cause a shudder in the consciousness of every libertarian in the country. Not only is "chemical castration" in the thoughts of legislators and judges across the country, it is also actually happening. California passed a law that mandates chemical castration as a condition of parole for repeat sex offenders and the discretionary chemical castration of paroled one-time sex offenders. Although this news may shock and surprise some, upon a closer examination and unraveling of the issues, chemical castration may not be such a bad idea after all and may be here to stay as part of American jurisprudence.

The term "chemical castration" is actually a misnomer. No permanent physiological alteration is required to carry out this procedure. Depo Provera, an FDA-approved birth control drug, is administered in weekly injections and serves to quell the sex drive of male sex offenders. This treatment, which will be explained further below, is not perfect however. The purpose of this article is to outline the debate surrounding the use of Depo Provera for "chemical castration" and the possible constitutional issues implicated by such use. To follow is an exploration of the nature and use of Depo Provera, followed by a discussion of the relevant constitutional issues. . . .

Depo Provera

Chemical castration is neither castration nor sterilization. Unlike actual castration, no permanent physical change is wrought in the body by the administration of Depo Provera to "chemically castrate" a sex offender. Depo Provera is an FDA-approved birth control drug that quells the sex drive of sex offenders; it lowers testosterone levels in males by decreasing androgen levels in the bloodstream. This, in theory, reduces the compulsive sexual fantasies of some types of sex offenders. Side effects from the drug have been rare and, according to Edward H. Fitzgerald, "are believed to be fully reversible with cessation of treatment."

Depo Provera treatment is a relatively recent response by some legislatures to help curb the recidivism rates of some types of sex offenders, most notably paraphiliacs, or those possessed of uncontrollable biological urges in the form of sexual fantasies that can usually only be satisfied by acting on the fantasy and succumbing to the compulsion. This capitulation often ends in the perpetration of a sex crime while the paraphiliac attempts to act out his fantasy. It is important to note that this form of chemical castration is theoretically only useful on this one particular type of sex offender—the paraphiliac. It should also be apparent that this drug regimen is only useful on male paraphiliacs since the effect of Depo Provera on females is to prevent conception (hence its use as birth control) and apparently has no effect on the sex drive. Studies have shown that through the use of such a regimen of weekly Depo Provera injections, paraphiliacs' recidivism rates drop substantially from upwards of 90% to as low as two percent. . . .

Chemical Castration as a Condition of Probation and/or Parole

Courts retain significant discretionary power when it comes time to grant a suspended sentence and probation to a convicted criminal in lieu of an actual prison sentence. Parole boards enjoy similar powers. Although a judge is supplied with a pre-sentence report and a sentence recommendation from the prosecutor, he or she still retains final say over the actual sentencing of the convict. It will now be possible for judges in chemical castration jurisdictions to condition probation (or parole boards to condition parole) on the convict accepting chemical castration. The convict is thus faced with the choice of going to prison (or staying there) or accepting the terms of probation, terms that include chemical castration. This choice may seem like a Hobson's choice when one considers the often gruesome consequences of keeping child molesters in general prison populations, but there are still a few important issues worth discussing.

First, critics may argue that there is not much of a choice between probationary chemical castration and prison, and that informed consent issues implicate themselves at this point. However, a prisoner's freedom of choice is not being violated in such a scenario. Although the available options may seem somewhat constraining, there is a legitimate choice to be made and the prisoner must voluntarily make that choice. A lack of informed consent could only be charged if the convict were to refuse to accept the treatment and it was subsequently forced upon him. To ensure that such claims do not arise, the orderly administration of chemical castration would have to be carried out in a manner consistent with the dictates of informed consent jurisprudence, with the convict knowing exactly what it is he is consenting to undergo.

Second, probation and parole are merely devices used by the legislature and the penal system to reward good behavior or nonviolent offenders in an effort to ease the strain on the already vastly overcrowded prison system. Probation and parole serve to preserve resources in a system that is already bursting at the seams. Although statutory mandates can be the source of rights, it seems safe to say that probation and parole are privileges, not rights. A convict forfeits his or her right to walk free among society upon conviction of a crime and may do so as part of probation or parole only through the good graces of the criminal justice system and the legislature. In sum, although the choice of accepting the terms of probation or parole may seem like a Hobson's choice, this choice would not even be available but for the current pressures on the penal system and the handiwork of past legislators. Convicts would be left to serve out their sentences in prison with no option for probation or parole. . . .

First Amendment Implications

Several constitutional issues are implicated by a policy of chemical castration, but perhaps none are as fundamental or vital to the notion of a free society as those embodied in the First Amendment to the United States Constitution. Of the rights that may be infringed by a regimen of Depo Provera treatment, the most notable is the convict's freedom of expression.

Freedom of expression is a fundamental right guaranteed by the First Amendment. That amendment has been held to encompass all manner of human expression and thought. It could be argued that chemical castration inhibits a convict's freedom of expression by repressing his or her compulsive sexual fantasy, thereby constituting an insidious form of governmental mind control. Though this argument has some intrinsic merit, it fails to recognize the goal of such a chemical regimen—returning the paraphiliac's thought process to normal. Moreover, it has never been held that any of our fundamental rights are absolute. People have no more freedom to yell "Fire!" in a crowded movie theater than women have a right to have an abortion in the third trimester of their pregnancies. In addition, the government has always been free to impose time, place, and manner restrictions on the exercise of these rights.

Given these universally held considerations and restrictions on certain fundamental rights, freedom of expression is also constrained by certain governmental or societal interests. The perverted fantasies of child molesters and the compulsive sexual fantasies of other paraphiliacs are arguably within this category of unprotected expression. Although the government has not, until this point, been able to effectively control the thoughts of its citizenry, the effect with regard to chemical castration is merely to return the offenders to a state of normalcy. Once freed from such compulsive fantasies, paraphiliacs have an increased capacity to ponder other topics and to engage in a wider variety of activities that were previously impossible due to the constraints placed on their minds by their overwhelmingly compulsive fantasizing.

Eighth Amendment Implications: Cruel and Unusual Punishment

Perhaps the most widely recognized and vehemently held position against chemical castration is that it violates the "cruel and unusual punishment" clause of the Eighth Amendment. Physical castration would certainly qualify as cruel and unusual and has been held to violate certain standards of decency and normalcy that we as a society have relegated to more barbaric times. Thus, the argument goes, chemical castration is in effect no different from physical castration because it robs men of the ability to procreate (another fundamental right) and effectively castrates them. This argument, however, is flawed in several ways.

Chemical castration does not physically alter the body other than by suppressing the production of testosterone, keeping it at "safe" levels. Aside from some reports of dangerous side effects, Depo Provera has not been causally linked to anything more serious than headaches and nausea, which are rare. Depo Provera is even safer under the conditions of probation or parole since the treatment is only carried out for a relatively short span of time (the length of the probationary period). Most studies that have linked the drug to more serious side effects speculate that such effects may take place if the drug is used on a long-term basis, something usually not an issue when dealing with probationary periods, typically of short duration.

The U.S. Supreme Court has handed down several indicators to help determine whether a punishment is cruel and unusual. The first threshold element required to apply cruel and unusual punishment analysis is to determine whether the act is indeed punishment or whether it is treatment. Many medical procedures, such as Depo Provera treatments, are subject to this treatment versus punishment argument. If a medical procedure is a legitimate treatment being used in good faith as a preventative or curative measure, then it should not be deemed punishment and is thus not subject to Eighth Amendment analysis. Depo Provera treatment should fall under this protective umbrella. . . .

International Castration Success

Some of the most striking results of experiments in using chemical castration . . . come from studies in Denmark and Switzerland, where voluntary chemical castration reduced recidivism rates from 50 percent or higher to substantially less than 10 percent. In a widely cited statement, one Danish sex offender raved, "My sex fantasies, which once made me a criminal, are gone. Watching a pornographic movie is like watching the evening news."

Craig Turk, *New Republic*, August 25, 1997.

Chemical castration in the context of probationary conditions should be viewed as a legitimate medical treatment that not only attempts to effectively rehabilitate paraphiliacs, but also serves to fulfill the compelling state interest of protecting children from child molesters. The goal of requiring chemical castration during probationary periods is to treat the offender in order to restore that person to health while allowing him to remain in the community and to maintain communal ties and employment. There must be some psychological counseling in conjunction with the Depo Provera injections to help the paraphiliac master his compulsions. Without such counseling, chemical castration as a rehabilitative device is impotent since treatments eventually cease as the probationary term ends. . . .

Fourteenth Amendment Implications

Not the least of the Fourteenth Amendment concerns implicated by chemical castration is the fundamental right to procreate. Critics of Depo Provera argue that the paraphiliac's right to procreate is violated by having to take a drug that for all intents and purposes creates what Fitzgerald calls "erotic apathy" and effectively eliminates all desire and ability to engage in normal sexual relations. This concern, however, is baseless since it has been shown that paraphiliacs undergoing treatment with Depo Provera can engage in intercourse and conceive children in much the same way as other people. Even though the convict may be subject to this "erotic apathy," the ability to procreate is maintained and the sex drive is not entirely squelched, just diminished to the point where compulsion becomes controllable. . . .

The liberty interest protected by the Fourteenth Amendment has come to encompass a number of fundamental rights, including the rights to procreate and to privacy. Beyond these important rights loom another set of important, though perhaps less well known, principles or rights. Like the right of privacy, however, courts have never held the liberty interest to be absolute. Among the state interests that can trump an individual's liberty interest are protection of life, prevention of suicide, protection of third parties, and protection of the medical profession.

1. *Right to refuse medical treatment:* Courts have traditionally held that a person maintains a liberty interest in his or her own bodily well-being and that this interest includes the right to make decisions about what to do with one's own body. Along this line, courts have generally held that a per-

son does have a right to refuse medical treatment so long as that right does not intrude upon a legitimate governmental interest such as preserving life. . . . The discerning reader will note that the right to refuse medical treatment is the logical corollary to the right to consent to medical treatment.

Chemical castration is a form of medical treatment that is within a person's right to refuse. However, the difficulty arises when a weighing of this right and the government's interest in preventing child molestation is performed. To overcome the right to refuse medical treatment, the government must demonstrate a rational relation to a legitimate state interest, which in this case would be the prevention of child molestation, something well within the parameters of this guideline. A paraphiliac still retains some right to refuse chemical castration, however, by opting not to accept the terms of the probation or parole.

2. *Right to treatment and right to rehabilitation:* Courts have never recognized a fully conceived right to treatment for convicted sex offenders. Although courts have upheld some minimal treatment requirements for involuntarily committed mental patients, they have never upheld a requirement that the government must try to treat every criminal. This principle comes into play in the present situation if a convicted sex offender attempts to argue that the government must let him go free as long as he voluntarily undergoes chemical castration. Here the sex offender assumes a right to treatment that requires the government to step in and do everything it can to further his rehabilitation. However, it has never been held that the criminal justice system must subscribe to the rehabilitation model or even have that as one of its goals. . . .

Greater Protection for Society's Children

Chemical castration through weekly Depo Provera injections in combination with psychological therapy is a safe, effective way to drastically curb the recidivism rates of paraphiliacs. Though the California Penal Statute permitting the use of Depro Provera has its flaws, the idea of using chemical castration as a probation or parole condition is constitutionally sound and is gaining in popularity. If drafted properly and used effectively and responsibly, chemical castration legislation could provide one more alternative to ease the problem of recidivism in certain populations of sex offenders. Not only would such legislation ease the burden on already over-taxed prison resources, it would also provide far greater protection for society's children by breaking the cycle of compulsion in which many paraphiliac offenders find themselves. Chemical castration should be considered a constitutionally novel alternative for treating paraphiliac offenders and a way in which such convicts can be effectively rehabilitated. The previous efforts of the criminal justice system in attempting to remedy this serious social problem have been, at best, impotent.

> "The involuntary injection of drugs into
> the body of a defendant over an extended
> period of time . . . is highly problematic
> and perhaps dangerous."

Chemical Castration Is Unconstitutional and Often Ineffective

Larry Helm Spalding

Chemical castration involves the use of medroxyproges-terone acetate (also referred to as MPA or Depo Provera) to reduce the sex drive of sex offenders released on probation. Larry Helm Spalding maintains in the following viewpoint that laws permitting the practice of chemical castration, such as those enacted in Florida in 1997, are unconstitutional and ineffective. According to Spalding, such laws violate the sex offenders' constitutional right to reproduce, and constitute cruel and unusual punishment. Moreover, Spalding argues that chemical castration does not address the root causes of much sexual violence, such as hatred and the need to control others. Larry Helm Spalding is legislative staff counsel for the American Civil Liberties Union of Florida.

As you read, consider the following questions:
1. According to Spalding, what are some of the side effects of MPA?
2. What way does chemical castration fail the reasonable relationship test, according to the author?

Throughout history, castration has been used to punish sex offenders. By the late 1900s, most castration sentences were disallowed on appeal, and a relieved public lauded itself for living in more enlightened times. However, in Florida, the definition of "enlightenment" changed when, in 1997, the Florida Legislature overwhelmingly enacted chapter 97-184, Florida Laws, opening the door for "chemical castration" of sex offenders. The new statute mandates court-ordered weekly injections of a sex-drive-reducing hormone to qualified repeat sex offenders upon release from prison. It may also be administered to first-time sex offenders.

Child molesters, rapists, and other sex offenders are perceived as among the most vile members of society. It is not surprising, therefore, that the Legislature revived an ancient method of turning these condemned men into eunuchs. This time, however, the lawmakers advocated the use of drugs, not the surgeon's scalpel, to accomplish their objective. While medical advances have made chemical suppression of the sex drive possible as a treatment for some sex offenders, the procedure is not free from criticism by medical, psychological, and psychiatric professionals. Moreover, some, like the American Civil Liberties Union (ACLU), believe that court-ordered, mandatory chemical castration is unconstitutional.

This Article explores whether mandatory chemical castration is a medically acceptable and constitutionally permissible alternative to incarceration for sex offenders in Florida. . . .

The Wonder Drug: MPA

Florida's chemical castration statute permits sex offenders to elect physical castration, but it is unlikely that many defendants will choose this option. Although a number of European countries have used surgical castration as a punitive measure, the procedure has never been regarded with favor in the United States. Most Americans object to the procedure on humanitarian and civil liberties grounds such as cruel and unusual punishment.

Medroxyprogesterone acetate (MPA), the drug mandated by the Florida Legislature for use in chemical castrations, is more commonly known as Depo-Provera. The Food and

Drug Administration (FDA) originally approved the drug for irregular uterine bleeding, threatened miscarriage, and amenorrhea, or the absence of menstruation. Today, it is marketed world-wide as a female contraceptive.

The FDA has not approved MPA specifically for use in chemical castrations. Nonetheless, it is not considered an experimental drug and, therefore, can be prescribed by any physician under the FDA Guidelines relating to the "use of approved drugs for unlabeled indications." In men, the drug reduces the production of the hormone testosterone in the testes and the adrenal glands, and, therefore, reduces the level of testosterone circulating through the bloodstream. As testosterone levels drop, so does the putative sex drive in most men.

MPA has been used successfully with only one type of sex offender, the paraphiliac, who demonstrates a pattern of sexual arousal, erection, and ejaculation that is accompanied by a distinctive fantasy or its achievement. While MPA has proven successful for some paraphiliacs, there is considerable scientific opinion that the drug is not likely to have any meaningful influence on three other types of sex offenders who come within the purview of the new statute: defendants who deny the perpetration of the offense; defendants who admit the perpetration of the offense, but who blame their behavior on non-sexual or non-personal forces, such as drugs, alcohol, or job stress; and defendants who are violent and appear to be prompted by non-sexual factors, such as anger, power, or violence. However, the new statute makes no distinction among the four different types of sex offenders. . . .

When used on males, MPA effectively suppresses erections, ejaculations, and reduces the frequency and intensity of erotic thoughts. Side effects include increased appetite, weight gain of fifteen to twenty pounds, fatigue, mental depression, hyperglycemia, impotence, abnormal sperm, lowered ejaculatory volume, insomnia, nightmares, dyspnea (difficulty in breathing), hot and cold flashes, loss of body hair, nausea, leg cramps, irregular gall bladder function, diverticulitis, aggravation of migraine, hypogonadism, elevation of the blood pressure, hypertension, phlebitis, diabetic sequelae, thrombosis (leading to heart attack), and shrinkage of the prostate and seminal vessels. . . .

The new statute raises several constitutional issues, including possible violations of the right to refuse nonconsensual medical treatment, the right to privacy, the prohibition against cruel and unusual punishment, due process and equal protection, and double jeopardy.

Involuntary Treatment and Informed Consent

The Florida statute suggests that the Legislature intended to include a broad range of sex offenders within the purview of the statute. However, many doctors believe MPA should be administered to a more narrowly delineated class of persons. According to these doctors, the pivotal criterion in calculating the treatability of any sex offender is the patient's acknowledgment that his conduct is intolerable and beyond his control.

Moreover, according to health care professionals who have been at the forefront of advocating the use of chemical castration as an effective alternative to incarceration, successful treatment requires competent psychotherapy and close monitoring in addition to the administration of MPA. Regrettably, neither psychotherapy nor any other kind of treatment beyond the mandatory, weekly injection of the drug is mentioned in the new statute.

It appears that the Legislature, in enacting the chemical castration statute, has proceeded on the belief, or perhaps more accurately, on the *hope*, that administering a single drug—even involuntarily—can effectively alter abusive behavior in all categories of sexual offenders. However, given the statute's broad application to the four types of sexual offenders, each with different underlying causes for their exhibited criminal behavior, and the omission of the critical element of therapeutic counseling for those forced to undergo the procedure, it is difficult to conclude that the Legislature seriously viewed chemical castration as a form of treatment rather than punishment. To paraphrase the old truism about the duck: if it looks like punishment, if it operates likes punishment, and if the Legislature intended for it to be punishment, then it must be punishment.

Obtaining a defendant's informed, voluntary consent for the administration of any drug, particularly one that has never received FDA sanction for the legislatively mandated purpose, is not only sound medical practice, it is constitutionally required. The U.S. Supreme Court has recognized that an individual possesses a liberty interest that includes the right to withhold consent to intrusive medical treatment. Courts have also held that prisoners and competent patients involuntarily committed to state mental institutions do not forfeit their fundamental right to refuse non-consensual medical treatment. However, courts have also recognized that in the face of legitimate prison regulations to preserve prison safety and security met by reasonably related procedures, the rights of prisoners may be limited. A court must weigh the prisoner's decisional autonomy and bodily integrity interest against the nature of the government's compelling interest.

People Are More than Hormones

The idea that sex drive is related purely to biological predisposition and lacks conscious thought is unfounded scientifically and is threatening to individuals whose sexual behavior might be seen outside the realm of normal, says Daniel C. Tsang, a librarian at UC Irvine who wrote a detailed history of the drug [Depo Provera] in men for the *Journal of Homosexuality*.

"My objection is to the idea that you can control sexuality with chemicals. We are more than just our hormones," he says.

Shari Roan, *Los Angeles Times*, September 26, 1996.

In *Canterbury v. Spence*, the court stated that "[t]he root premise [to the doctrine of informed consent] is the concept, fundamental in American jurisprudence, that '[e]very human being of adult years and sound mind has a right to determine what shall be done with his own body.'" The question thus becomes whether court-ordered chemical castration of a defendant at the time of his release from confinement, as required by the new statute, is *voluntary*.

Chemical castration is an intrusive and invasive procedure with many known side effects and long-term health risks. Mandatory weekly drug injections qualify as an unjustified interference of a defendant's constitutionally protected rights, absent a demonstrated showing of a "compelling state interest." Protecting society from recidivist child molesters and rapists is unquestionably a compelling governmental interest. Nonetheless, given the paucity of evidence that chemical castration is an effective means of treatment for non-paraphiliacs and involuntarily-treated paraphiliacs, mandatory administration of MPA is not reasonably related or narrowly tailored to the state's legitimate goals of rehabilitation and public safety.

Proponents of chemical castration emphasize that because the offender can choose, at least in theory, to not submit to the procedure, the medical treatment is consensual. But the *choice* to discontinue the administration of MPA can result not only in a violation of probation, but also in an indictment for an additional second degree felony. Consequently, exercising the option to withdraw from the medical treatment, without the consent of the court, is no option at all. Given this reality, the choice cannot be held to be made freely, knowingly, or voluntarily.

The Right to Privacy

The U.S. Constitution does not prove an explicit right to privacy. The U.S. Supreme Court has, however, acknowledged an implied right to privacy under the Fourteenth Amendment. This fundamental guarantee protects an individual's decisional autonomy and right to bodily integrity with respect to decisions concerning childbearing and contraception.

State-mandated administration of an impotence-inducing hormone not only involves compelled medical care, but also invades the constitutionally protected right to privacy. Like forced sterilization and contraception, an order directing periodic injections of MPA implicates the rights of bodily integrity and reproductive autonomy. In *Skinner v. Oklahoma*, the Court acknowledged that the right to procreate represents one of the basic civil rights of humanity and that such a right is fundamental to the very existence and survival of the race.

The Court has expressed "great resistance to expand the substantive reach of [the Due Process Clause], particularly if it requires redefining the category of rights deemed to be fundamental." In this effort, the Court has rendered precise requirements for those rights that should be protected, insisting "not merely that the interest denominated as a 'liberty' be 'fundamental' . . . but also that it be an interest traditionally protected by our society." Yet, a finding by the courts that procreation is fundamental did not unduly jeopardize the reach of the Due Process Clause because "[t]he rights to conceive and to raise one's children have been deemed 'essential' . . . 'basic civil rights of man' . . . and '[r]ights far more precious . . . than property rights.'"

The Court in *Paul v. Davis* recognized that legislation infringing on the right of procreation invokes a heightened constitutional analysis. Chemical castration as a punitive measure for convicted sex offenders violates the right of procreative freedom. To render a convicted sex offender virtually impotent is to deprive him of his right to procreate, a right characterized in cases such as *Skinner* as "one of the basic civil rights of man." In addition, castration by periodic injections represents a more intrusive procedure than a vasectomy because it results in a diminution of the sex drive. While proponents of the new statute argue that the chemical castration procedure involves only a temporary interference with an individual's ability to reproduce, the individual's ability to procreate is still infringed upon during the period of treatment. Moreover, the new statute provides courts with the authority to order that the injections be administered for life.

Cruel and Unusual Punishment

Techniques outside the scope of traditional penalties, such as fines and incarceration, are constitutionally suspect. Courts have invalidated several medical treatments as cruel and unusual punishment and view with particular disfavor experimental, peculiar, and ineffective "therapies." In *Skinner*, Justice Robert H. Jackson wrote, "[t]here are limits to the extent to which a legislatively represented majority may conduct biological experiments at the expense of the dignity and personality and natural powers of a minority—even those who have been guilty of what the majority define as crimes."

In reasoning that echoes a cruel and unusual punishment analysis, the court in *People v. Gauntlett* struck down a sentence compelling a man convicted of a sexual offense to submit to MPA injections as an unlawful condition of probation and unauthorized by state law because MPA had not received FDA approval specifically for chemical castrations, and had not gained acceptance in the medical community as a safe and effective treatment for males. While chemical castration has yet to be analyzed pursuant to the federal Constitution, courts have held surgical castration to be violative of the Eighth Amendment's proscription against cruel and unusual punishment. In holding that a fine for assault and battery was within the sentencing parameters established by a Georgia statute, the court in *Whitten v. State* explained that quartering, burning, hanging in chains, and castration are cruel and unusual punishments. In *Davis v. Berry*, the court struck down an Iowa statute that authorized vasectomies for repeat felons as cruel and unusual punishment, and as violative of both equal protection and due process. The court distinguished vasectomy from surgical castration, but reasoned that the two procedures induced similar effects on the defendant. Vasectomy, like castration, was held to be cruel and unusual punishment because "the humiliation, degradation, and mental suffering are always present and known."

Due Process and Equal Protection

Although courts maintain great discretion in imposing terms of probation, all probationary conditions must meet the requirements of the reasonable relationship test. Probationary conditions must be reasonably related to the crime for which the offender was convicted, to the rehabilitation of the offender in order to prevent future criminality, or to the promotion of public safety. The imposed condition may not be overbroad in its application. The condition must also be narrowly tailored to meet the goal of rehabilitation "without unnecessarily restricting the probationer's otherwise lawful activities."

Chemical castration fails both prongs of the reasonable relationship test with regard to non-paraphiliacs and involuntarily-treated paraphiliacs. First, those who assert that the government's interest in protecting the public is met by removing an offender's ability to commit future sex crimes fail to recognize that continued incarceration is a more narrowly tailored means of furthering the state interest than chemical castration. Second, because the non-paraphiliac's conduct is often motivated by anger and hatred rather than sexual desire, a treatment that merely curbs sexual desire bears no reasonable relationship to the offender's criminal behavior. Third, application of chemical castration to all repeat offenders violates the requirement that a condition of probation not be overbroad. Because chemical castration is an ineffective treatment for non-paraphiliacs, it cannot meet its intended goal in this class of sex offenders where the purpose of probation is to rehabilitate. Fourth, the statute strips the courts of any discretion to make an individual determination of the suitability of MPA treatment for repeat sexual offenders. Periodic, indefinite injections are mandated for repeat sex offenders, regardless of how dangerous the drug may be and whether the procedure offers any effective treatment. The statute's mandate is particularly inappropriate for a sentence that requires the ingestion of a drug that may be totally ineffective and may inflict serious side effects. Fifth, chemical castration does not necessarily prevent future criminality because the treatment does not address the offender's violent tendencies and thus does not curb an offender's urge to commit acts of sexual battery. In fact, some experts fear that chemical castration will, because of the shame it instills, augment the violent nature of some offenders. Moreover, because non-paraphiliac offenders are motivated not by sexual drive, but by intense feelings of hatred and hostility, the procedure may cause an increase in the occurrences of this type of sexual battery.

Finally, there is the issue of gender. On its face, the statute is gender neutral. The consequences, however, are not. Both males and females who commit sexual battery are theoretically subject to the statute. MPA was designed to be used by women as a safe contraceptive. It has no effect on the female sex drive. In contrast, MPA has been legislatively mandated for use in a biological experiment designed to curb the sex drive of men convicted of sexual battery. The long-term physical and psychological effects of the administration of the drug are unknown.

In sum, the diagnosis of the cause of a particular sexual battery is difficult and requires a comprehensive evaluation of the driving forces behind the behavior as well as the emotional responses to the behavior. The new statute does not take into account the complexities of the causes of sexual battery. Instead, it provides the court with a single solution—the involuntary injection of drugs into the body of a defendant over an extended period of time—which is highly problematic and perhaps dangerous. . . .

Misidentifying Root Causes

The reasoning advanced for the enactment of Florida's chemical castration statute is that rehabilitation of sex offenders and the safety of Florida's citizens are sufficient justifications for establishing chemical castration as a condition of release for convicted sex offenders. In response, the medical experts, whom the Legislature chose to ignore, maintained that rehabilitation and reduction in recidivism can only occur when the drug addresses the specific behavioral abnormality of the particular sex offender, the treatment is voluntary and not coerced, the individual genuinely wants to address his aberrant behavior, and there is extensive therapeutic counseling and monitoring of the individual.

How can Floridians be safe and secure if the court-ordered drug treatment is administered to those whose motivation is not sex, but rather violence, hatred, and control, on the mistaken belief that it is likely to have a measurable impact on the root causes of the defendant's criminal behavior? How can Floridians have confidence in a legislative enactment, adopted under the guise of rehabilitation, that mandates a medical practice that is condemned as experimental and even irresponsible by medical authorities?

> "*Sex offender registration and notification laws . . . can provide a stronghold against the dangerous criminals who live among us.*"

Community Notification Laws Can Help Reduce Sexual Violence

Alan D. Scholle

Community notification laws—also known as sex offender registries or "Megan's Laws," after seven-year-old Megan Kanka, who was raped and murdered by her neighbor in 1994—require that members of a community be notified when a sex offender is being released into their neighborhood. Alan D. Scholle argues in the following viewpoint that community notification laws, when used in conjunction with community education and cooperation, can help reduce sexual violence. According to Scholle, such laws can be used to apprehend suspected sex offenders and help law enforcement agencies solve sex crimes. Alan D. Scholle writes for the *FBI Law Enforcement Bulletin*.

As you read, consider the following questions:
1. As related by the author, what agencies usually maintain sex offender registries?
2. What is the Jacob Wetterling Act, according to Scholle?
3. As reported by the author, what is the difference between passive and active community notification?

Although sex offender registration requirements vary according to state laws, some common features exist in registries across the country. In most states, the state criminal justice agency or board (e.g., the state police or state bureau of investigation) maintains the state's registry. Sex offenders register at local law enforcement or corrections agencies, which then forward the information to the state's central registry. Registry information typically includes the offender's name, address, date of birth, social security number, and physical description, as well as fingerprints and a photograph. In Iowa, registration includes information about the sex offense convictions that triggered the registration requirement. At least eight states also collect samples for DNA identification.

Registration Requirements

Most state laws require that both juvenile and adult offenders register only if their conviction occurred after the law's effective date, although some states, such as Minnesota, require that offenders register after they get charged with a sexual offense. Offenders receive notice of the registration requirement from the court or registry agency. In Iowa, offenders can contest the registration requirement by filing an "application for determination" with the state Department of Public Safety.

Usually, offenders must register within a certain number of days following their release from custody or placement on supervision. The type of offense requiring registration varies according to state law but must comply with the 1994 Jacob Wetterling Act, which mandates registration for sex crimes against minors and violent sex crimes. For example, in Iowa, qualifying offenses include criminal sexual offenses against minors; sexually violent offenses; sexual exploitation; aggravated offenses, including murder, nonparental kidnapping, or false imprisonment; manslaughter; and burglary, if sexual abuse or attempted sexual abuse occurred during the commission of the crime, as well as other relevant offenses, such as indecent exposure.

The registration requirement lasts at least 10 years, with some states requiring lifetime registration for all or some offenses. Some states allow offenders to petition the court for a reduction. Iowa law requires lifetime registration for offenders deemed "sexual predators" by the courts and for any registered offenders who get convicted of a subsequent sexual offense.

Most states make it a criminal offense to knowingly fail to register or report subsequent changes in information, such as the registrant's name or address. Public officials in Iowa verify annually the addresses of all registrants.

Notification Features

Sex offenders may have to register, but if the public does not know it, the law means little. It may have cost Megan Kanka her life.[1] In response, Megan's Law allows for release to the public certain information about registered sex offenders. State agencies generally have guidelines or administrative rules regarding what information they will release to whom and how they will disseminate it.

The most basic form of notification, sometimes referred to as "passive notification," allows inquiring citizens to access registry information at their local law enforcement agencies. In Iowa, citizens must complete a request for registry information form at their local police or sheriff's department and provide the name of the person being checked and one of three identifiers: address, date of birth, or social security number. If the agency finds the person on the registry, it can release certain information about the offender; however, federal guidelines prohibit states from releasing the identities of victims. Employers also may check on potential employees. Since Iowa's law took effect in 1995, members of the public have made 14,923 requests for registry information.

Several states provide a toll-free number for citizens to call to obtain information. California and New York operate 900-number services for inquiries. Many states allow public access to sex offender registry information through Internet sites maintained by criminal justice agencies. This informa-

---

1. Seven-year-old Megan Kanka was raped and murdered by her neighbor in 1994. Community notification laws are often referred to as "Megan's Laws" in her honor.

tion usually includes offenders' photographs, biographical data, and information about their previous sex offenses.

Monitoring Sex Offenders

Increased monitoring of sex offenders fosters greater cooperation between law enforcement and other criminal justice agencies charged with supervising these individuals during probationary or parole terms. For example, periodic contacts between the Registration Enforcement and Compliance Team (REACT) (which monitors sex offenders for the Los Angeles Police Department) and subjects on parole for past sex crimes increase the number of unannounced checks and aid parole officers burdened with large caseloads. This additional monitoring often uncovers violations of release conditions. . . .

Recent REACT contacts with parolees include a twice-convicted child molester, who targeted kindergarten-age girls. The parolee assured officers that he could manage his sexual attraction to children. Although he complied with registration requirements, REACT officers initiated surveillance due to the severity of his past crimes and propensity to re-offend. Within days, officers observed the parolee slowly driving by an elementary school playground. This violation of a parole condition prohibiting him from going near a school sent the parolee back to prison.

Bernard C. Parks and Diane Webb, *The FBI Law Enforcement Bulletin*, October 2000.

In addition to these forms of passive notification, a number of states allow government agencies to disseminate information about registered sex offenders to vulnerable individuals and organizations. Using this process of "active notification," officials may choose to notify prior victims, landlords, neighbors, public and private schools, childcare facilities, religious and youth organizations, and other relevant individuals or agencies. Most officials reserve communitywide notification for only the most dangerous sex offenders. Communitywide notification usually involves using the media and such public forums as neighborhood association and other community meetings.

States have various methods for determining which offenders qualify for active notification. In Florida and Montana, state courts determine which sex offenders pose the greatest threat to the community and target them for active notification. A number of states, including Iowa, allow criminal justice officials or state registry review boards to assess the offender's level of risk, then law enforcement officials, prosecuting attorneys, or corrections personnel typically make the notification. Louisiana requires that registered sex offenders themselves notify neighbors within 1-square block in the city or a 3-mile radius in rural areas. . . .

A Stronghold Against Dangerous Criminals

A 1988 survey of 420 criminal justice agencies across the country found that a majority of the reporting agencies considered registration laws a useful tool in apprehending suspected sex offenders. Moreover, sex offender registries provide law enforcement agencies with an additional tool to help them investigate unsolved sex crimes or other violations, such as burglary, kidnapping, or murder, when sexual assault occurs as part of the offense. Iowa law enforcement officials have access to a list of registered sex offenders by county that they can use to identify potential suspects in unsolved cases. . . .

Legislators and criminal justice officials recognize that registration and notification laws generate controversy and have inherent limitations and drawbacks. In fact, registration and notification of sex offenders are merely pieces of a comprehensive law enforcement strategy to enhance public safety. Criminal justice officials and the public need to work together to reduce sexual violence in their communities.

It has been said that good fences make good neighbors. Yet, when sex offenders move into the neighborhood, residents may need more. Sex offender registration and notification laws, in conjunction with community education and cooperation, can provide a stronghold against the dangerous criminals who live among us.

"Community notification has little, if any, impact on the likelihood that a convicted sex criminal will strike again."

Community Notification Laws May Be Ineffective

Joshua Wolf Shenk

Community notification laws—also known as "Megan's Laws" after a New Jersey girl who was sexually assaulted and murdered by a neighbor in 1994—require that neighbors be notified when a sex offender is released into their community. In the following viewpoint, Joshua Wolf Shenk claims that such laws are ineffective at deterring released sex criminals from offending again. In addition, he argues that since most child sexual abuse is not committed by strangers, the fear and suspicion created by such laws is unnecessary. Community notification laws can also lead to vigilantism, he contends. Joshua Wolf Shenk is an author, essayist, and storyteller whose work has appeared in numerous magazines, including *Harper's Magazine* and the *American Prospect*.

As you read, consider the following questions:

1. How did Scott Lee Stoller get around community notification laws, according to the author?
2. As reported by Shenk, what percentage of Washington State sex offenders reoffended after Megan's Laws went into effect?

When Scott Lee Stoller, a convicted child molester, left prison in 1996, Seattle police notified his neighbors with a community meeting and a flier that called him "a high risk to reoffend." But that August, Stoller drove 10 minutes across Lake Washington to Redmond, where parents hadn't been warned of his violent past, and molested two girls, ages 5 and 6. "I don't count on notification to protect anybody," says Robert Hales, a Redmond detective who helped arrest Stoller. "But at least the public is aware that these individuals are living in their neighborhoods."

Do Megan's Laws Deter Criminals?

Washington State was the first in the country to pass a law requiring that communities be notified when a sex offender moves nearby. These laws—now known as "Megan's laws" after the New Jersey girl raped and murdered by her neighbor in 1994—got a big boost in the Supreme Court [in March 1998], when it refused to hear arguments that such civil actions constitute double jeopardy, or two punishments for the same crime.

But even if these laws are constitutional, a more basic question remains: Do they deter offenders? Evidence from Washington State's eight-year experience with the law suggests that community notification has little, if any, impact on the likelihood that a convicted sex criminal will strike again. According to a 1995 state study, in the period before the state's "Megan's law," 22 percent of sex offenders who had been arrested went out again and committed sex crimes. After the law went into effect, the number hardly budged: It was 19 percent.

The Biggest Worry

Officials say that notification is mostly useful as a way to educate the public. Robert Shilling, a Seattle detective who has run hundreds of community meetings, says he uses them to make a broader point. "I always say, 'This person is not your biggest worry. Your biggest worry is the person you don't know about, yet.'" By raising the profile of sex crimes, notification laws have put pressure on police to apprehend suspects and the justice system to mete out tougher punishment.

But heightened awareness can also lead to increased fear and suspicion. Sandra Yudilevich, the nurse who examined Stoller's most recent victims, wonders about the long-term consequences of injecting such worry into children's lives: "It's an unknown quantity. I can foresee problems, particularly in homes where protectiveness is really overdone."

COMMUNITY NOTIFICATION

Kirk. © Kirk Anderson. Reprinted with permission.

Polls bear out changing attitudes about safety: About half of Washington parents, for example, say they're less likely than before the law was passed to leave their kids alone—even with a baby sitter. Roxanne Lieb, an expert on notification laws at the Washington Institute for Public Policy, calls it a rare sight to see younger children walking home from school alone or even waiting for the bus.

Most Sex Offenders Are Not Strangers to Their Victims

Such fear of strangers may be misplaced. Skeptics of notification point out that fewer than 10 percent of sex criminals are strangers to their victims. The most common category of abuse is within the family. Some even argue that Megan's laws could have an adverse affect, silencing victims of incest for fear that those molesting them—their parents or siblings—will become pariahs. This is a particular concern in Louisiana, which is the only state that requires sex offenders to notify the community themselves. Judges have even required offenders to wear special clothing or sandwich boards announcing their past crimes.

One common effect of such disclosure is to make communities rise up against individual offenders. Even in Washington State, where police publicly vow to protect the right of past offenders to be left alone, more than 30 acts of vigilantism have been recorded since the notification law took effect. Most dramatically, in 1993, arsonists burned down the home to which a paroled child rapist was supposed to be released.

Many offenders' daily lives are affected, too. One recently released child molester bought a boat with his wife but was rejected by dozens of different docks in the Seattle area before finding one that would lease him space. Kevin, who asked to be identified by his first name only, says he supports community notification because "the best indicator of future behavior is past behavior." But he noted that even intense scrutiny is often not enough to stop many offenders: "No external factor is going to keep me from reoffending—not the program, not my wife, not God. Only me."

| *"[Rape shield] laws kept a woman from being treated like a criminal during the trial against her rapist."*

Rape Shield Laws Are Necessary

Mary E. Bahl

Rape shield laws keep a woman's sexual history from being brought up in court during a rape trial. Mary E. Bahl contends in the following viewpoint that these laws were designed to prevent courts from asking an alleged rape victim humiliating questions about her sex life that could call into question her moral character and, in turn, her testimony against the defendant. Bahl admits that numerous high-profile sexual abuse cases have called into question the fairness of disallowing evidence that could help the defendant, but she argues that such cases do not negate the need for rape shield laws. On the contrary, Bahl claims that although such laws may need to be reworked, they are still essential to protect rape victims. Mary E. Bahl writes for *Impact Press*, a bimonthly sociopolitical magazine.

As you read, consider the following questions:
1. How has society changed since 1970, in Bahl's opinion?
2. According to the author, what did the e-mail transcripts in the Oliver Jovanovic case indicate about the acuser?
3. In Bahl's view, why does the Jovanovic case fail to prove that rape shield laws are unnecessary?

I magine this: you're a young woman living in a large city in 1970. One night, you're out on a date with a man. He wants sex; you don't. He becomes more and more insistent until he finally becomes violent, forcing you to the ground and raping you. After he leaves, you go directly to the police station to report the crime. When you speak to the police, they keep asking you questions: Did you have sex with this man before? How many sexual partners have you had in the past? Did you invite him into your apartment? What were you wearing?

Somehow you get past this line of humiliating questions and the accused rapist is brought to trial. When you are put on the stand, the defending attorney asks you many of the same questions, questions about your past relationships. He produces evidence that you've had a couple of sexual relationships before dating the man who raped you. He makes the case that since you've had sex before, you must have been "asking for it". The charges against the young man are dismissed.

Rape: One of the Most Feared Crimes

Of all the crimes that exist, one of the most feared is rape. It's violent, it's humiliating, and it invades a person in a way that no other crime can. In an ideal case, when a rape victim went to the police to report the crime committed against her (rape victims are usually women), she would be given a sympathetic ear, a prompt medical examination, and the full assistance of the law to prosecute the rapist. But even as recently as 20 to 30 years ago, this was not often the case.

Fortunately, there was change. Starting in the 1970s, most states in the U.S. started passing "rape shield laws". The purpose of these laws was to keep a woman's sexual history from being brought up in court during a rape trial. Juries therefore couldn't use this history against a woman. These laws kept a woman from being treated like a criminal during the trial against her rapist.

Society is much different than it was back in 1970, however. Pre-marital sex is much more common and women are less likely to be judged for having sex. Women who have been raped are much more likely to report the crime and the rapists are much more likely to stand trial. According to the

Rape, Abuse and Incest National Network (RAINN), rapes and sexual assaults declined more than 17 percent between 1995 and 1996. Due to the increasing awareness about rape and society's changing attitudes towards women, there are some who believe that the rape shield laws are no longer necessary and should be repealed. Some of these people believe that rape shield laws keep an accused rapist from receiving a fair trial and that the laws are discriminatory against men.

The Jovanovic Case

The 1998 trial of Oliver Jovanovic, a student at Columbia University, is an illustration of the anti–rape shield law viewpoint. Jovanovic met a female Barnard College student in an online chat room. They kept an online correspondence going for six months before meeting for a date in November 1996. During the date, she and Jovanovic went back to his apartment where she removed her clothes and allowed Jovanovic to tie her to a futon. The Barnard student claims that Jovanovic then held her forcibly for 20 hours, torturing and sodomizing her. When she was finally let go, the Barnard student had Jovanovic arrested for rape.

Prevalence of Rape from Three Studies

Violence Against Women Survey (1), National College Risk Health Risk Behavior Survey (2), U.S. Naval Recruit Health Study (3)

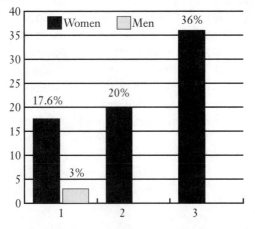

National Violence Against Women Prevention Research Center, 2000.

The twist in the case came when the lawyers for Jovanovic claimed that the Barnard student had many discussions about sadomasochism (S&M) with Jovanovic and expressed a desire to engage in that activity with Jovanovic. The lawyers had transcripts of all of the two parties' emails to each other so as to prove that the Barnard student consented to the activities. The Barnard student claimed under oath that she never discussed any interests in S&M with Jovanovic.

Even though Jovanovic had the email transcripts as evidence that the Barnard student had wanted S&M activities to take place, Jovanovic was forbidden from submitting these transcripts in court because of the rape shield laws of the state. Since many of the transcripts described the Barnard student's past sadomasochistic relationships, they were considered part of her sexual history and therefore inadmissible in court. Jovanovic was convicted of rape, but he has since filed an appeal.[1]

People who want rape shield laws repealed say that the Jovanovic case is a clear example of abuse of the laws and how it turns rape into a "his word against hers" situation. On the other hand, there is one obvious point to be made: even if the Barnard student had expressed an interest in and an initial consent to sadomasochistic activities with Jovanovic, she is still allowed to change her mind when the activities commence. Even if she had consented to be tied up and "tortured", she still should have been free to stop at any time (the S&M community uses "safe words", words that indicate to all parties involved that the activity must stop immediately). If Jovanovic had continued the sexual contact after she had told him to stop, he would have been guilty of raping her. Even if someone has a history of engaging in a particular sexual activity, especially one that is seen as controversial, he or she is not immune to rape or assault.

The Marv Albert Case

Another trial where rape shield laws did not assist the accused rapist is the 1997 much-publicized sportscaster Marv Albert

---

1. Oliver Jovanovic's conviction was overturned. New York's highest court found that acting justice William Wetzel had misapplied the New York rape shield law.

trial. Accused of assault and battery after biting his mistress during a sexual encounter, Albert and his lawyers wished to bring witnesses to testify that his lover had a history of falsely accusing men of assault and rape. The judge denied this request, since any mention of the victim's past sexual history was protected under the rape shield laws. However, Albert's mistress was permitted to call as a witness a few of Albert's ex-lovers to testify to his "strange" sexual habits.[2]

It would seem after viewing two cases that rape shield laws can prevent a man accused of rape from defending himself in court, as he is entitled to do under the law. Those who want the laws repealed say that this is a case of reverse discrimination and sexism towards men. This may well be true in these and other cases. But the fact remains that many victims of rape and sexual assault are victimized once again in court by charges that their past sexual histories make them "loose" and "having asked for it". Even though society's attitudes towards women, sex and rape are changing for the better, those changes are coming slowly. Old attitudes have kept rapists from getting punished, but old laws may prevent accused rapists (who are, after all, still innocent until proven guilty) from defending themselves against false accusers. Rape shield laws may still be a necessity, but they may need some rethinking and reworking so that true justice may be served consistently.

2. Marv Albert pleaded guilty to misdemeanor assault.

> *"Current uses of the rape shield law may violate the defendant's Sixth Amendment right to confront witnesses against him."*

Rape Shield Laws Are Unfair

Cathy Young

Rape shield laws restrict the discussion of the accuser's sexual past in sexual abuse trials. In the following viewpoint, Cathy Young contends that such laws may be unconstitutional because they deny defendants the right to properly defend themselves. According to Young, there have been numerous high-profile cases in which defense attorneys were not allowed to submit relevant evidence about the accuser's sexual history, such as a stated willingness to engage in sadomasochism. In consequence, rape shield laws have resulted in the unfair conviction of countless men. Cathy Young is vice president of the Women's Freedom Network and author of *Ceasefire: Beyond the Gender Wars*.

As you read, consider the following questions:

1. How did rape shield laws originate, according to Young?
2. As reported by the author, what inadmissible evidence in the Marv Albert trial might have helped the defendant win his case?
3. What information about the accuser in the Charles Steadman case does the author argue should have been admissible?

In April 1998, Oliver Jovanovic, a 31-year-old doctoral candidate in microbiology at Columbia University, was convicted of kidnapping and sexually abusing a 22-year-old Barnard College student he had met in an Internet "chat room." "The defense did not do enough to defend Oliver," a juror said after the verdict. In fact, the defense was hamstrung by the misapplication of a law, intended to protect victims from being dragged through the mud, which instead has been used to withhold evidence that could exonerate the accused.

Jovanovic and the Barnard student went on a date after meeting in an America Online chat room in 1996 and exchanging electronic mail. At his apartment, by her own account, the young woman let herself be stripped and tied up; she claimed that Jovanovic then kept her bound, against her will, for 20 hours and sexually tortured her. The defense argued that what happened was consensual. This argument, however, was crippled by Judge William Wetzel's decision—based on New York's "rape shield" law, which restricts the use of the accuser's sexual past—to exclude portions of the e-mail dealing with sadomasochistic sexual activity.

The Relevance of Sexual History

Rape shield laws, now on the books in every state, originated in the feminist overhaul of rape law in the 1970s. The reforms were directed at real injustices: Once, juries were commonly instructed that they could consider an accuser's lack of chastity as detracting from her credibility, and defense lawyers could grill a woman about her sexual partners. Such inquiries are now rightly perceived as not only cruel but irrelevant: A woman's promiscuity doesn't prove that she consented to sex with a particular man.

Yet sometimes sexual history is directly relevant to consent and credibility. In the Jovanovic case, the defense contends that the law ended up shielding perjury. The young woman testified that in her correspondence with Jovanovic, she had never given any indication that she was interested in sadomasochism—a statement that the e-mail excluded from trial would have called into doubt.

Such suppression of vital evidence seems blatantly unfair, particularly when a defendant is risking a sentence of up to

25 years in prison. It should be noted that the judge also excluded as "prejudicial" the testimony of an ex-girlfriend who says Jovanovic subjected her to a sexual attack similar to the Barnard student's account. One may debate whether her story should have been admissible, considering that she never reported the alleged attack and has no medical record of injuries. But at least Judge Wetzel was more even-handed than Arlington, Virginia, Circuit Court Judge Benjamin Kendrick, who presided over the trial of sportscaster Marv Albert in 1997.

More Suspect Cases

Mr. Albert was charged with sexually assaulting and biting a longtime lover, who identified herself after the trial as Vanessa Perhach. During the trial, Judge Kendrick allowed another woman to testify that Mr. Albert had also attempted to assault and bite her. The defense was kept from introducing evidence that reportedly showed Ms. Perhach had a pattern of behaving vindictively toward men who broke up with her (as Mr. Albert was doing), that her methods of revenge included false accusations of criminal acts, and that biting was a part of her sexual repertoire (which would have undercut the prosecution argument that the bite marks were proof of assault).

Neo-Victorian Paternalism

While defense lawyers should not be empowered to dredge up an accuser's past just to humiliate her, evidence about it should be treated in the same way as other evidence: If it's relevant and useful and obtained legally, it's generally admissible. Special rules related to a woman's sexual behavior smack of neo-Victorian paternalism.

Cathy Young, *Washington Post*, October 20, 1997.

With his kinky proclivities exposed to a national audience and his defense hog-tied, Mr. Albert was pressured into pleading guilty to misdemeanor assault. Many commentators, even those sympathetic to victims' rights, were appalled by what they saw as a perversion of laws protecting victims. But this was not an aberration. In a number of less notorious cases, exculpatory evidence has been withheld from the jury because it was related, sometimes indirectly, to the accuser's past sexual behavior.

The jury in the 1993 trial of Charles Steadman, an 18-year-old Wisconsin man charged with sexually assaulting a 23-year-old woman, never learned that the complainant was herself facing criminal charges of sex with underage boys (she was later convicted). The defense wanted to argue, not implausibly, that this gave the woman a motive for a false complaint. She might have thought that being a victim might improve her situation. Or she might have worried that if her encounter with Steadman—with whom she had first gotten involved when *he* was a minor—became known, it would aggravate her legal troubles. The judge, however, ruled that the charges pending against her could not be mentioned, since they had to do with past sexual activities. Steadman was convicted and sentenced to eight years in prison.

Rape Shield Laws May Violate the Constitution

Legal scholars—including such feminists as Vivian Berger of Columbia University—have warned that current uses of the rape shield law may violate the defendant's Sixth Amendment right to confront witnesses against him and to produce evidence in his favor. So far, appellate courts have not been sympathetic to these concerns. In several states, including Iowa, Pennsylvania and Washington, courts have held that even excluding an earlier false allegation of rape by the accuser does not deny the accused a fair trial.

In 1994, the U.S. Court of Appeals for the Seventh Circuit upheld the attempted-rape conviction of Lonnie Stephens, who was barred at trial from giving his version of the events: that the woman became enraged at him because, during sex, he mentioned that a male friend had told him she liked a particular sexual position. While troubled by this hobbling of Stephens's right to defend himself, the court was more worried about creating a loophole defendants could use to smuggle in the victim's sexual past.

Jovanovic's attorneys are planning to appeal his conviction.* This case could prove to be a good opportunity to re-

---

*Oliver Jovanovic's conviction was overturned on appeal. New York's highest court found that acting justice William Wetzel had misapplied the New York rape shield law.

examine the constitutionality of rape shield laws when they result in the exclusion of relevant evidence. Champions of victims' rights have argued for years that the truth-seeking function of a trial is impeded when key evidence against the defendant is dismissed on a legal technicality. It is impeded just as much when key evidence that helps the defendant is barred out of a misguided paternalism toward women.

Periodical Bibliography

The following articles have been selected to supplement the diverse views presented in this chapter.

American Criminal Law Review	"Megan's Law and the Protection of the Child in the Online Age," Summer 1998.
Robert Bilbrey	"Civil Commitment of Sexually Violent Predators: A Misguided Attempt to Solve a Serious Problem," *Journal of the Mississippi Bar*, November/December 1999.
Suzanne Fields	"More than Mourning for Megan," *Washington Times*, June 26, 1997.
Rael Jean Isaac	"Put Sex Predators Behind Bars, Not on the Couch, *Wall Street Journal*, May 8, 1998.
Michelle Johnson	"Notification Dilemmas: Megan's Law Spawned Flurry of State Acts, but Implementation Proves Problematic for All," *Quill*, September 1998.
Kelly McMurry	"Fewer Sex Offenders on Community Release Programs than Other Criminals," *Trial*, April 1997.
Bernard Parks and Diane Webb	"Sex Offender Registration Enforcement: A Proactive Stance to Monitoring Convicted Sex Offenders," *FBI Enforcement Bulletin*, October 2000.
Todd S. Purdum	"Registry Laws Tar Sex-Crime Convicts with Broad Brush," *New York Times*, July 1, 1997.
Lamar Stonecypher	"A Strange Cure for Rape," August 2001. www. kudzumonthly.com.
Clarence Thomas	"*Kansas v. Leroy Hendricks*," Supreme Court Collection, 1997. http://supct.law.cornell.edu.
Craig Turk	"Kinder Cut: A Limited Defense of Chemical Castration," *New Republic*, August 25, 1997.
Cathy Young	"Excluded Evidence: The Dark Side of Rape Shield Laws," *Reason*, February 2002.

For Further Discussion

Chapter 1

1. Randy Thornhill and Craig T. Palmer rely on facts about male and female reproduction to support their argument that rape is a natural, male biological urge. In contrast, Barbara Ehrenreich discusses rape's negative impact on the children produced by rape to make her point that rape cannot be seen as a reproductive strategy. In your opinion, which viewpoint uses evidence most convincingly? Please explain.

2. Fear Us describes specific portrayals of women in pornography to bolster its argument that such depictions promote sexual violence against women. The American Civil Liberties Union discusses several studies to support its claim that there is no correlation between pornography and violence against women. Which type of evidence do you find more persuasive, and why?

3. Alyn Pearson contends that male-dominated cultures socialize men to sexually abuse women. What evidence does Pearson provide to support her argument? Do you find her argument persuasive? Why or why not?

4. Barbara Crossette explains that women have always been exploited during wartime. However, whereas in the past women were raped because they were viewed as spoils of war, today they are raped in order to devastate their cultures, which often consider women's fidelity and virginity as central to their identity. In your opinion, is wartime rape more or less devastating to victims today than it was in the past? Please explain, using details from the viewpoint.

5. The *Economist* claims that many U.S. schools transfer employees who are accused of child sexual abuse to other districts rather than deal with the problems involved in bringing charges against them. What does the magazine recommend to make schools safer for children? If you were on a committee whose goal was to protect children from sexual predators, what further recommendations would you make to your school's administration? What would you tell parents and children?

Chapter 2

1. Neil Gilbert argues that many researchers exaggerate the prevalence of rape by examining a variety of smaller studies with different methodologies and presenting the cumulative results as evidence of a serious problem. In light of Gilbert's criticism,

how persuasive do you find Mary P. Koss's analysis of recent studies and the conclusions she draws from them? Please explain your answer using specifics from both authors' texts.

2. Thomas D. Oellerich contends that no one really knows the prevalence of child sexual abuse. However, Rebecca M. Bolen and Maria Scannapieco draw concrete conclusions about the extent of child sexual abuse from their analysis of existing studies. Examine the methods used by Bolen and Scannapieco in their analysis. Are you convinced by the figures they present regarding the extent of child sexual abuse? Please explain.

3. Catholic bishop Wilton D. Gregory denies claims such as those made by Andrew Sullivan that child sexual abuse by priests is widespread. He asserts that there are only a few priests who have engaged in such abuse and claims that the Catholic Church is noted for its leadership in combating sexual violence. In your opinion, does the fact that Gregory is a Catholic bishop help or hurt his argument? Please explain your answer.

Chapter 3

1. To support her claim that violence against women is a serious problem, Martha T. McCluskey provides an example of the abuse she suffered at the hands of fraternity members at Colby College. In order to illustrate how such public avowals of female victimization reinforce stereotypes of women, Katie Roiphe gives examples of victims' speeches at "Take Back the Night" marches. In your opinion, which author uses evidence more convincingly? Please explain your answer.

2. Both James Lein and Rael Jean Isaac discuss the nature of memory in their viewpoints. Lein claims that memories of trauma are less subject to distortion than other memories and, even when repressed for years, can be recalled later with accuracy. On the other hand, Isaac argues that intense emotional experiences are the most likely to be forgotten and that memories of abuse are apt to be distorted by the imagination. Which author's discussion of memory do you find most persuasive? Why?

3. To support his argument in favor of using the battered woman syndrome as a legal defense, Douglas A. Orr claims that most battered women are unable to leave the abusive relationship and so must be given the legal right to defend themselves, even if it means killing the abuser. Conversely, Joe Wheeler Dixon supports his argument against the battered woman syndrome defense by discussing laboratory experiments showing that animals who had "learned helplessness" did not react with rage and ag-

gression. In consequences Dixon concludes that women *are* able to leave abusive relationships and should never be permitted to murder. In your opinion, which author's discussion of helplessness is most convincing? Explain.

Chapter 4

1. Christopher Meisenkothen claims that chemical castration of sex offenders on parole does not violate their fundamental right to procreate. However, Larry Helm Spalding argues that chemical castration does indeed violate sex offenders' right to reproduce. Examine how each author supports his argument and determine which you think makes a more convincing case. Please explain your answer, using quotes from both viewpoints.

2. Both Alan D. Scholle and Joshua Wolf Shenk use studies to support their arguments. Scholle uses a 1988 survey of 420 criminal justice agencies to bolster his contention that community notification laws help law enforcement personnel apprehend suspected sex offenders. In contrast, Shenk discusses a 1995 study of Washington State's experience with community notification laws to argue that such laws do little to deter sex offenders. Examine how each author uses these studies to strengthen his argument. Which author do you find more convincing, and why?

3. Cathy Young uses the Oliver Jovanovic case to illustrate why rape shield laws are unfair to the accused. However, Mary E. Bahl claims that the Jovanovic case cannot be used to argue against rape shield laws. Please examine the way that each author uses the case and explain which argument you find more persuasive.

Organizations to Contact

The editors have compiled the following list of organizations concerned with the issues debated in this book. All of them have publications or information available for interested readers. For best results, allow as much time as possible for the organizations to respond. The descriptions below are derived from materials provided by the organizations. This list was compiled upon the date of publication. Names, addresses, phone and fax numbers, and e-mail and Internet addresses of organizations are subject to change.

American Civil Liberties Union (ACLU)
132 W. 43rd St., New York, NY 10036
(212) 944-9800 • fax: (212) 921-7916
website: www.aclu.org

The ACLU is a national organization that works to defend Americans' civil rights guaranteed in the U.S. Constitution. The organization opposes censorship of all types, including the censorship of pornography.

Canadian Association of Sexual Assault Centres (CASAC)
77 E. 20th Ave., Vancouver, BC, Canada V5V 1L7
(604) 867-2622 • fax: (604) 876-8450
e-mail: headoffice@casac.ca • website: www.casac.ca

CASAC is a group of sexual assault centers that have come together to implement the legal, social, and attitudinal changes necessary to prevent, and ultimately eradicate, rape and sexual assault. The association acts as a force for social change regarding violence against women at the individual, institutional, and political levels.

Center for the Prevention of Sexual and Domestic Violence (CPSDV)
2400 N. 45th St., Suite 10, Seattle, WA 98103
(206) 634-1903 • fax: (206) 634-0115
e-mail: cpsdv@cpsdv.org • website: www.cpsdv.org

CPSDV is an interreligious educational resource center that works with both religious and secular communities throughout the United States and Canada to address the issues of sexual abuse and domestic violence. The center offers workshops concerning sexual misconduct by clergy, spouse abuse, child sexual abuse, rape, and pornography. Materials available from the CPSDV include the quarterly newsletter *Working Together* and the *Journal of Religion and Abuse*.

Center for Women Policy Studies (CWPS)
1211 Connecticut Ave. NW, Suite 312, Washington, DC 20036
(202) 872-1770 • fax: (202) 296-8962
e-mail: cwps@centerwomenpolicy.org
website: www.centerwomenpolicy.org

CWPS is an independent feminist policy research and advocacy institution established in 1972. The center studies policies affecting the social, legal, health, and economic status of women. Available publications include fact sheets on violence against women and girls and the reports *Violence Against Women as Bias-Motivated Hate Crime: Federal and State Laws* and *Violence Against Women and Girls.*

Emerge: Counseling and Education to Stop Domestic Violence
2380 Massachusetts Ave., Suite 101, Cambridge, MA 02140
(617) 547-0979
e-mail: infor@emergedv.com • website: www.emergedv.com

Emerge is a victim-advocacy organization that works to prevent domestic violence, including sexual violence, by providing training workshops to counselors and counseling services to batterers. It also conducts research and disseminates information. Publications available from Emerge include the articles "Counseling Men Who Batter: A Pro-feminist Analysis of Treatment Models" and "The Addicted or Alcoholic Batterer."

False Memory Syndrome Foundation (FMSF)
1955 Locust St., Philadelphia, PA 19103-5766
(215) 940-1040 • (800) 568-8882 • fax: (215) 940-1042
e-mail: mail@fmsonline.org • website: www.fmsonline.org

Members of the foundation believe that many "delayed memories" of sexual abuse are the result of false memory syndrome (FMS), which they say is caused by therapists' mistakenly implanting false memories of traumatic experiences in the minds of their patients. The foundation seeks to discover reasons for the spread of FMS, works for the prevention of new cases, and aids FMS victims, including those falsely accused of sexual abuse. The foundation publishes the *FMS Foundation Newsletter* and various working papers and distributes articles and information on FMS.

Family Research Laboratory (FRL)
University of New Hampshire
126 Horton Social Science Center, Durham, NH 03824-3586
(603) 862-1888 • fax: (603) 862-1122
website: www.unh.edu/frl

FRL is an independent research unit devoted to the study of the causes and consequences of family violence. It also works to dispel myths about family violence through public education. It publishes numerous books and articles on violence between men and women, spouse/cohabitant abuse, marital rape, and verbal aggression. The organization's website offers a complete listing of available materials, including the article "Child Sexual Abuse and Pornography: Is There a Relationship?" and the book *Four Theories of Rape in American Society: A State-Level Analysis.*

Incest Survivors Resource Network International (ISRNI)
PO Box 7375, Las Cruces, NM 88006-7375
(505) 521-4260 • fax: (505) 521-3723
e-mail: ISRNI@zianet.com • website: www.zianet.com/ISRNI

ISRNI is a Quaker-operated networking and educational resource center dedicated to the prevention of incest. ISRNI offers numerous publications, sponsors conferences, and operates a helpline staffed solely by incest survivors.

National Center for Missing and Exploited Children (NCMEC)
699 Prince St., Alexandria, VA 22314
(703) 274-3900 • toll-free hotline 1-800-THE-LOST
e-mail: ncmec@cis.compuserve.com • website:
www.missingkids.org

NCMEC is a private organization funded by the Department of Justice. The center serves as a clearinghouse information on missing and exploited children and coordinates child protection efforts with the private sector. The center also maintains a 24-hour hotline that callers can use to report child pornography and sightings of missing children. Available publications include guidelines for parents whose children are testifying in court, child safety information, and books such as *Children Traumatized in Sex Rings.*

National Coalition Against Censorship (NCAC)
275 Seventh Ave., New York, NY 10001
(212) 807-6222 • fax: (212) 807-6245
e-mail: NCAC@netcom.com • website: www.ncac.org

NCAC is an alliance of organizations committed to defending freedom of thought, inquiry, and expression by engaging in public education and advocacy on the national and local levels. The coalition promotes the belief that the censorship of violent and sexual materials represses intellectual and artistic freedom. NCAC maintains a library of information dealing with First Amendment issues. It publishes the quarterly *Censorship News*.

National Coalition for the Protection of Children and Families
800 Compton Rd., Suite 9224, Cincinnati, OH 45231
(513) 521-6227 • fax: (513) 521-6337
e-mail: ncpcf@nationalcoalition.org
website: www.nationalcoalition.org

Formerly known as the National Coalition Against Pornography, the coalition is an alliance of civic, business, religious, health care, and educational groups working to stop the violence that they believe is promoted by obscenity and child pornography. It assists citizens in enforcing laws against child pornography and obscenity; it also helps draft legislation to initiate or strengthen existing anti-obscenity laws. The coalition's publications include *Children, Pornography, and Cyberspace* and *Pornography: A Human Tragedy*.

National Coalition of Free Men
PO Box 582023, Minneapolis, MN 55458-2023
e-mail: ncfm@ncfm.org • website: www.ncfm.org

The coalition's members include men seeking "a fair and balanced perspective on gender issues." The organization promotes men's legal rights in issues such as false accusation of rape, sexual harassment, and sexual abuse. It conducts research, sponsors educational programs, maintains a database on men's issues, and publishes the bimonthy *Transitions*.

National Institute of Justice (NIJ)
U.S. Department of Justice
National Criminal Justice Reference Service
PO Box 6000, Rockville, MD 20849-6000
(800) 851-3240
e-mail: askncjrs@ncjrs.org • website: www.ojp.usdoj.gov/nij

The NIJ, the research and development agency of the U.S. Department of Justice, was established to prevent and reduce crime and to improve the criminal justice system. It provides studies and statistics on child rape victims, child victimizers, and violence against women. Among its publications are the reports "The Criminal Justice and Community Response to Rape" and "When the Victim Is a Child."

NOW Legal Defense and Education Fund
395 Hudson St., New York, NY 10014
(212) 925-6635 • fax: (212) 226-1066
website: www.nowldef.org

The NOW Legal Defense and Education Fund is a branch of the National Organization for Women (NOW). It is dedicated to the eradication of sex discrimination through litigation and public education. The organization offers a list of publications on rape, incest, and sexual abuse, as well as a legal resource kit on child sexual abuse.

Office for Victims of Crime Resource Center
PO Box 6000, Rockville, MD 20849-6000
(800) 627-6872
website: www.ncjrs.org

Established in 1983 by the U.S. Department of Justice's Office for Victims of Crime, the resource center is a primary source of information regarding victim-related issues. It answers questions by using national and regional statistics, research findings, and a network of victim advocates and organizations. The center distributes all Office of Justice Programs (OJP) publications, including *Female Victims of Violent Crime* and *Sexual Assault: An Overview*.

People Against Rape (PAR)
6296 Rivers Ave., Suite 307, North Charleston, SC 29406
(843) 745-0144 • fax: (843) 745-0119
website: www.people-against-rape.org

People Against Rape primarily seeks to help teens and children avoid becoming the victims of sexual assault and rape by providing instruction in the basic principles of self-defense. PAR further promotes self-esteem and motivation of teens and college students through educational programs. Publications include *Defend: Preventing Date Rape and Other Sexual Assaults* and *Sexual Assault: How to Defend Yourself*.

Rape, Abuse, and Incest National Network (RAINN)
635-B Pennsylvania Ave. SE, Washington, DC 20003
(800) 656-HOPE • fax: (202) 544-3556
e-mail: rainnmail@aol.com • website: www.rainn.org

RAINN operates America's only national hotline for victims of sexual assault. The hotline offers free, confidential counseling and support twenty-four hours a day, from anywhere in the country.

Sex Information and Education Council of the U.S. (SIECUS)
130 W. 42nd St., Suite 350, New York, NY 10036-7802
(212) 819-9770 • fax: (212) 819-9776
e-mail: SIECUS@siecus.org • website: www.siecus.org

SIECUS is a clearinghouse for information on sexuality, with a special interest in sex education. It publishes sex education curricula, the bimonthy newsletter *SIECUS Report*, and fact sheets on sex education issues. Its articles, bibliographies, and book reviews often address the role of sex education in identifying, reducing, and preventing sexual violence.

Survivor Connections (SC)
52 Lyndon Rd., Cranston, RI 02905-1121
e-mail: scsitemail@cox.net
website: www.angelfire.com/ri/survivorconnections

Survivor Connections is an activist organization for survivors of sexual assault. It provides referrals to attorneys, therapists, and peer support groups. The organization also seeks to educate the public about legislation affecting survivors and encourages criminal prosecution and civil claims against perpetrators. A quarterly newsletter, the *Survivor Activist*, is available to the general public.

Survivors of Incest Anonymous (SIA)
PO Box 190, Benson, MD 21018
(410) 893-3322

Established in 1982, Survivors of Incest Anonymous is a twelve-step self-help recovery program for victims of incest. The organization provides national and international support groups, bulletins, and speakers; it also publishes the pamphlets *Incest: The Family Tragedy* and *Must We Forgive?*

Victoria Men's Centre
PO Box 8082, Victoria, BC V8W 3R7 Canada
(250) 370-4636
website: http://victoria.tc.ca/Community/MensCentre

The Victoria Men's Centre is the physical representation of a supportive men's network. The center works to support men and women who are actively working to achieve equality. It also works to promote the male role in parenting and a positive image for men as role models. The organization aims to provide men with alternatives to violence in relationships.

VOCAL/National Association of State VOCAL Organizations (NASVO)

7485 E. Kenyon Ave., Denver, CO 80237

(303) 233-5321 • fax: (303) 770-5096 • (800) 745-8778

VOCAL (Victims of Child Abuse Laws) provides information, research data, referrals, and emotional support to those falsely accused of child abuse, including sexual abuse. NASVO maintains a library of research on child abuse, focusing on legal, psychological, social, and medical issues, and will provide photocopies of articles for a fee. It publishes the monthly *NASVO/VOCAL Colorado Newsletter.*

VOICES in Action (Victims of Incest Can Emerge Survivors)

PO Box 13, Newtonsville, OH 45158

(800) 7-VOICE-8

e-mail: voices@voices-action.org • website: www.voices-action.org

VOICES in Action assists victims of childhood sexual abuse through support, networking, education, and promoting public awareness. The organization offers workshops, audiotapes of conference presentations, and the bimonthly newsletter the *Chorus.*

The Women's Center

46 Pleasant St., Cambridge, MA 02139

(617) 354-8807

e-mail: wmnscntr@attbi.com

The Women's Center provides women with the resources and support they need to emerge from conditions of domestic violence, sexual abuse, poverty, discrimination, social isolation, and degradation. The center developed and runs the Boston Area Rape Crisis Center and provides free counseling services to hundreds of low-income, uninsured women.

Bibliography of Books

David Archard   *Sexual Consent.* Boulder, CO: Westview Press, 1998.

Frank R. Ascione and   *Child Abuse, Domestic Violence, and Animal Abuse:*
Phil Arkow, eds.   *Linking the Circles of Compassion.* West Lafayette, IN: Purdue University Press, 1999.

Jeffrey R. Benedict   *Athletes and Acquaintance Rape.* Thousand Oaks, CA: Sage Publications, 1998.

C. Brooks Brenneis   *Recovered Memories of Trauma: Transferring the Present to the Past.* Madison, CT: International Universities Press, 1997.

Dante Cicchetti and   *Theory and Research on the Causes and*
Vicki K. Carlson, eds. *Consequences of Child Abuse and Neglect.* Cambridge, MA: Cambridge University Press, 1989.

Walter S. DeKeseredy   *Woman Abuse on Campus.* Thousand Oaks, CA:
and Martin D. Schwartz Sage Publications, 1998.

Donald Alexander   *More than Victims: Battered Women, the*
Downs   *Syndrome, and the Law.* Chicago: University of Chicago Press, 1996.

Andrea Dworkin   *Life and Death: Unapologetic Writings on the Continuing War Against Women.* New York: Free Press, 1997.

Lori B. Girshick   *Woman-to-Woman Violence: Does She Call It Rape?* Boston: Northeastern University Press, 2002.

Roy Hazelwood and   *Dark Dreams: Sexual Violence, Homicide and the*
Stephen G. Michaud   *Criminal Mind.* New York: St. Martin's Press, 2001.

T. Walter Herbert   *Sexual Violence and American Manhood.* New York: Harvard University Press, 2002.

James F. Hodgson and   *Sexual Violence: Politics, Practices, and Challenges*
Debra S. Kelley, eds. *in the United States and Canada.* Westport, CT: Praeger, 2002.

Ronald Holmes and   *Current Perspectives on Sex Crimes.* Thousand
Stephen T. Holmes,   Oaks, CA: Sage Publications, 2002.
eds.

Philip Jenkins   *Pedophiles and Priests: Anatomy of a Contemporary Crisis.* New York: Oxford University Press, 1997.

James R. Kincaid   *Child-Loving: The Erotic Child and Victorian Culture.* New York: Routledge, 1992.

James R. Kincaid   *Erotic Innocence: The Culture of Child Molesting.* Durham, NC: Duke University Press, 1998.

Lawrence Kramer	*After the Lovedeath: Sexual Violence and the Making of Culture*. Berkeley: University of California Press, 2000.
Sharice A. Lee	*The Survivor's Guide: For Teenage Girls Surviving Sexual Abuse*. Thousand Oaks, CA: Sage Publications, 1998.
Ronald F. Levant and Gary R. Brooks	*Men and Sex: New Psychological Perspectives*. New York: John Wiley, 1997.
Sandra E. Lund and Beth Leventhal	*Same-Sex Domestic Violence*. Thousand Oaks, CA: Sage Publications, 1999.
Wendy McElroy	*XXX: A Woman's Right to Pornography*. New York: St. Martin's Press, 1995.
Richard Ofshe	*Making Monsters: False Memories, Psychotherapy, and Sexual Hysteria*. New York: Charles Scribner's Sons, 1994.
Michele Antoinette Paludi, ed.	*The Psychology of Sexual Victimization: A Handbook*. New York: Greenwood Publishing Group, 1999.
Nancy Venable Raine	*After Silence: Rape and My Journey Back*. New York: Crown Publishers, 1998.
Claire M. Renzetti and Charles Harvey Miley	*Violence in Gay and Lesbian Domestic Partnerships*. New York: Haworth Press, 1997.
Diana E.H. Russell	*Dangerous Relationships: Pornography, Misogyny, and Rape*. Thousand Oaks, CA: Sage Publications, 1998.
Diana E.H. Russell and Rebecca M. Bolen	*The Epidemic of Rape and Child Abuse in the United States*. Thousand Oaks, CA: Sage Publications, 2000.
Gail Ryan and Sandy Lane	*Juvenile Sexual Offending*. San Francisco: Jossey-Bass, 1997.
Joseph Sandler and Peter Fonagy, eds.	*Recovered Memories of Abuse: True or False?* Madison, CT: International Universities Press, 1998.
Martin D. Schwartz and Walter S. DeKeseredy	*Sexual Assault on the College Campus: The Role of Male Peer Support*. Thousand Oaks, CA: Sage Publications, 1997.
Lawrence J. Simon	*Murder by Numbers: Perspectives on Serial Sexual Violence*. New York: Athena Press, 2002.
Randy Thornhill and Craig T. Palmer	*A Natural History of Rape: Biological Bases of Sexual Coercion*. Cambridge, MA: MIT Press, 2000.
Cheryl B. Travis	*Evolution, Gender, and Rape*. Cambridge, MA: MIT Press, 2003.
Cheryl B. Travis and Jacquelyn W. White	*Sexuality, Society, and Feminism*. Washington, DC: American Psychological Association, 2000.

Index